It's about them...Not you!

By Todd Cencich

Winning communication equals winning results

Copyright © 2012 by Todd Cencich
Cover Design by Torch Press inc.
Back cover photo by Patrick Sweeney

Copyright © 2012 Todd Cencich. All rights reserved.

Unless otherwise indicated, all materials on these pages are copyrighted by Todd Cencich. All rights reserved. No part of these pages, either text or image may be used for any purpose other than personal use. Therefore, reproduction, modification, storage in a retrieval system or retransmission, in any form or by any means, electronic, mechanical or otherwise, for reasons other than personal use, is strictly prohibited without prior written permission.

Published by Lulu Press Inc.
3101 Hillsborough St
Raleigh, NC 27607
919.447.3290
www.Lulu.com

Library of Congress Cataloging-in-Publication Data

It's About Them...Not You! – ID: 13080679

Cencich, Todd
It's About them...Not You! ; Transform your life and career by applying these principles to your everyday life / Todd Cencich

ISBN 978-1-300-03559-6

Printed and Bound in the United States of America

This book is dedicated to my precious children,

Valerie Lyn & Troy Christopher

Table of Contents

Introduction 8

Chapter 1 – About them.. 14

Chapter 2 - About you 26

Chapter 3 - Negotiating 35

Chapter 4 - About Goals 43

Chapter 5 - Conversation 51

Chapter 6 - Listening.. 58

Chapter 7 - Presenting Your Idea.................................... 65

Chapter 8 - Questions 74

Chapter 9 - Why Relationships Matter More than Facts 85

Chapter 10 - Dreams 93

Chapter 11 - Connect The Dots....................................... 104

Chapter 12 – Your Words 113

Chapter 13 - Not Everyone is Like You 119

Conclusion 126

Table of Contents

Introduction 8

Chapter 1 – About them.. 14

Chapter 2 - About you 26

Chapter 3 - Negotiating... 35

Chapter 4 - About Goals 43

Chapter 5 - Conversation 51

Chapter 6 - Listening.. 58

Chapter 7 - Presenting Your Idea.................................... 65

Chapter 8 - Questions 74

Chapter 9 - Why Relationships Matter More than Facts 85

Chapter 10 - Dreams... 93

Chapter 11 - Connect The Dots..................................... 104

Chapter 12 – Your Words 113

Chapter 13 - Not Everyone is Like You 119

Conclusion 126

Introduction

By nature, everyone is concerned about their own wants, what's in it for them, and how they can benefit from a given situation. However, when you are in contact with someone else, the other person is equally concerned about what is in it for them. Empathy, the ability to identify with another's feelings, viewpoint, and attitude is a learned skill. During conversations I'm intrigued when people feel compelled to talk about themselves. To me it's strange behavior. They are with themselves all day long, and yet, when they get in front of another individual, they revert to talking about themselves.

I was at my favorite lunch spot and I bumped into a couple of sales representatives I used to work with. They came over to say hello. One of them could not shut up about how awesome they are, all the success they have and how their lives couldn't be any better. It's funny because I don't remember it that way but their version was sort of humorous, so I let them go on. So after about 10 minutes of non-stop blather, they finally said, "So how are you?" We chatted for a little bit and then said our goodbyes.

As I thought about what transpired, I thought to myself; how remarkable it was that people whom I haven't seen in over a year, walked up and basically couldn't stop pumping themself up like a tire on a bicycle. I guess they were just as hollow as the space that filled that tire as well.

Why do people do that? What is it that makes people so self-absorbed and self-centered? Don't they think it's weird to just walk over and brag about their self-proclaimed success? And the thing that's comical is that I got wind afterward that it was highly exaggerated. C'mon! So why do people feel compelled to focus so intensely on themselves?

Part of the problem stems from the age in which we live. Our society encourages immediate gratification and people inadvertently become self-absorbed into their own little world. The end result is that people compare themselves with others and don't want to be overshadowed.

A contributing factor is the utilization and fascination with technology. We are never going to get away from the fact that the use of technology is only going to grow. Younger generations grow up with computers, wireless phones and speedy digital technology that gives them what they want instantly. The days of waiting for information are long gone and the need for speed abounds.

WHERE WERE YOU BEFORE COMPUTERS DOMINATED YOUR LIFE?

Maybe you can't remember. How often do you see people on their phones at the airport staring at that little screen as if it is telling them what to do next? I have been to numerous trade shows and seminars where several thousand sales professionals are in attendance, and what does everyone do the moment there is a break in the action? Well, can you guess? If you said, "check that little device that you can't live without", also known as a smart phone, you are correct and are on the right track.

How does technology affect our interaction with people? It diminishes it and turns otherwise normal people into zombies glued to their phones like a scene from "Night of the Living Dead",

So what about our children who are used to using computers, smart phones and other gadgets? Do you think they have lost some of what is important in human relations because it has been replaced by devices? Maybe. I know for sure that is doesn't help.

My point (and the premise of this book) is that communication with another human being is becoming a lost art and is being overshadowed by these cool gadgets. Now, I'm certainly not suggesting we throw away these hip and useful devices. But, anytime we are in the company of another person, we have the opportunity to communicate and connect in a way that is unique. And *IF* we are effective, it has the potential to be memorable and impactful. Don't you want to be remembered? Sure, who doesn't. And obviously we want to be remembered in a positive light.

It's About Them is taking the focus off of yourself and directing it to others. Stepping out of your shoes and wearing someone else's. It means that we leave our cell phone alone for 5 minutes and truly engage with another person.

One evening just before dusk I was talking with a neighbor when I saw three teenagers walking down the street. As they drew nearer I noticed that all three of them were texting as they were walking. They weren't talking, or even paying much attention to where they were going. The irony struck me that most people define being "social" by their activity on the internet, yet, they were ignoring the people they were with.

There is a humorous commercial that depicts a man and woman finally alone at a restaurant where they have a chance to talk. However the husband has his mobile device hidden where he can keep up with a sporting event on demand. The wife quickly becomes annoyed because she has to share the man's attention with his device (which by the way, is extremely slick). While the situation may be sort of humorous, sadly, it is all too true and it happens all the time.

No matter what setting we find ourselves where it involves people, the topics in this book can help improve your interaction skills and give you a different perspective with which to approach others. So, whether you are in a sales or professional position, or whether you want to effectively communicate with your children, ***It's About Them***, can be a beacon in an otherwise dimly lit path of interacting with other human beings.

It's not about you or what you want, it is truly about them. You will find that when you focus on others, the more freely they will interact with you. You will get resolution quicker, be perceived as more friendly, and you will get what you want because you helped them get what they want.

1

About Them

    Them. Some people wrestle with getting the attention off of themselves. The truth is that people are conditioned to focus on themselves. Many look inward rather than outward. We are still in the "me" generation because people's attention is so overtly on themselves. Now there is a time to focus on yourself and what you want, but when you are face to face with another individual or group of individuals it is your chance to focus on them. You should view it as a golden opportunity to make a connection with another person and gain from their insight and perspective.

    In order to effectively communicate with others, we must redirect our focus from us to them. If you desire meaningful interactions, get in the "them" habit to learn things. Those ideas may change your life. Any time we are with another person we have the occasion to gain from their viewpoint and grow.

This concept isn't limited to an active negotiation process, but whenever you are conversing with another human being. So why do people have trouble behaving this way? Peel the onion back a bit and go a little deeper. The closer you get to the core, the more you will find that our instinct for survival is basically a way of preserving our *self*.

CHALLENGE:

THE NEXT TIME YOU ARE IN A CASUAL CONVERSATION, RESIST THE TEMPTATION TO MAKE IT ABOUT YOU. MAYBE THEY ARE TELLING YOU A STORY ABOUT THEIR KIDS SOCCER GAME AND YOUR INSTINCT IS TO JUMP IN WITH YOUR VERSION. RESIST THE TEMPTATION. INSTEAD, ASK ANOTHER QUESTION ABOUT THEIR CHILD OR EXPERIENCE. *WHAT DID YOU NOTICE?*

I remember a conversation a long time ago where I was in the middle of a philosophical debate. We both had strong arguments to support our principle and each of our cases was airtight. I would say something, he would say something – it was a battle of wit and words. As the conversation went on for hours and both sides refusing to give in, we finally decided to end the discourse. We agreed to disagree and went our separate ways. I had mixed feelings at the time because on one hand, I stood my ground and didn't budge, but on the other hand I was disappointed that I didn't persuade the other to see my viewpoint, because I was the one that was right.

As I look back on that conversation a few things stood out to me. First, I was **talking at** this person and not **with** them. Repeatedly I restated my position, saying the same thing from a different angle. Oh, and conviction, man I had it! Second, I was not listening. Yes I know, that is shocking. As the other person was talking I wasn't listening to what they were saying. I was thinking about what I was going to say to repudiate their comments (later in this book, there is an entire chapter on listening). Third, I treated their opinion like it was wrong and I was totally right. I was polite, but I didn't even try to consider that maybe part of it was right. Fourth, I did NOT consider **why** they thought that way. Sometimes if we can understand why they think the way they do, or at least understand how it's possible to think a certain way, then we can at least identify with them on some level.

That conversation was a failure as far as I was concerned. The more I thought about it I wondered why I could not get them to see my point of view. This took place many years ago, and at the time I hadn't yet developed the skill necessary to connect with someone that didn't share the same values as mine. So it was just a bunch of banter back and forth. I might as well have been talking to a rock.

Do you talk to rocks? You do if you talk AT people rather than talking with them.

Ben Franklin wrote of conversation in his autobiography (pg. 27), *"And as the chief ends of conversation are to inform, or to be informed, to please or to persuade, I wish well-meaning sensible men would not lessen their power of doing good by a positive assuming manner that seldom fails to disgust, tends to create opposition, and to defeat every one of their purposes for which speech is given us, to wit, giving or receiving information, or pleasure…"*

So discussion is a two way street and we must be open to the exchange of ideas. It's got to be a free flowing exchange of thought and more than just supposition. Our discussion is not based on simple feeling. It has to be grounded by some factual basis or experience.

Going back to my conversation, I was so busy trying to hammer my ideals by force, I didn't consider for one second the concept that the other person was sharing with me. I was closed minded to any opinion outside my own way of thinking. Sometimes when we are closed minded and simply accept what we know as fact without supporting information, we don't consider that there may be additional information or another way of looking at something. Also, consider the possibility we may not know the entirety of a subject. Someone else may have information that may add to what we believe, therefore strengthening our core beliefs. I'm not saying that we should fully swallow every idea that comes our way. But I am saying that it's important that we don't ever stop learning. When you close yourself off from learning, you no longer have the opportunity to grow and will become stagnant.

When we are putting this in the context of being, "about them", we ought to have the mindset that polite conversation should be two-way, and not talking to rocks. (not that the other person is a rock, but if we are talking AT someone, we might as well be.)   The old adage goes, "people don't care how much you know until they know how much you care". AMEN!

In conversing with others, it is vital that we take an interest in what they bring to the table. This is true of a family member, neighbor, co-worker, business associate, grocery clerk, friend, classmate, spouse, child, teacher, or that person we bump into at the gym. Everyone thinks their values are right, so you had better respect that. Everyone we interact with on a regular basis may not see thing from our viewpoint. THANK GOD! Like that great line from the movie Caddyshack, where one of the characters was concerned that he might not get a scholarship to college. The man who was in charge of awarding the scholarship replied, "Well, the world needs ditch diggers too." I don't care who you are, that's funny. But it brings up a great point. If we all did the same thing and thought the same way, how boring would the world be? Very boring indeed, even if everyone was exactly like you.

If we focus on ourselves, we will miss those hidden gems that ordinary people overlook. Everyone has something unique that they can offer. Some more than others, but still, you can gain something or learn from anyone. So we should not be so discriminatory in our view of other people or look down on them because we don't see things from their perspective. Perhaps if you were exposed to the things that they were, you would think the like they do. Maybe if you went through the same challenges and hardships they went through, maybe you too would stumble as they have.

CHALLENGE:

THE NEXT TIME YOU ARE FEELING LIKE YOU CANNOT SUCCEED, MENTALLY REFUSE TO GIVE IN. ASK WINNING QUESTIONS OF YOURSELF. LOOK FOR REASONS WHY YOU CAN SUCCEED AND SUCCESS WILL FOLLOW YOU.

A key in conversing with others is not to prejudge. I had a new sales job where I was loaded up with a large number of accounts. As I began meeting with a few of them I was initially discouraged. I aired my grievances with my manager and told him I felt that these accounts were some of the worst and how unfair it was to me to have to bear this burden. He heard me out and then told me that I really knew nothing about these accounts and that I should not prejudge them. In fact he told me that in his opinion I was far superior to any salesperson that had called on them previously and that he needed someone with my ability to handle them. I left his office feeling like a champion. I called on those accounts for the next few months and found opportunities that others overlooked and had an extremely successful run. Looking back, my boss didn't stop me when I began complaining or tell me that I wasn't a company man. He conversed with me and heard what I was saying and told me what I needed to hear. He didn't prejudge me either. He heard what I was saying and turned my attention in a direction it should have been in.

If you have been around for any length of time, you have probably judged people without really knowing them and then after you got to know them, you wonder how you ever thought that way about them. Or, maybe you initially thought someone was really special and after you get to know them, aaahhh, not so much.

Internal prejudice may keep us from connecting with someone. Find out what is inside someone before making gross assessments about them. Get to the **why** of their beliefs. Find out what makes them tick. It's human nature, but we tend to judge other people by their actions, and ourselves by our intentions. Why not give *them* the same benefit of the doubt?

You'll be amazed at how much you can learn from other people, if you allow them to speak and you hear them rather than talk at them. I've been in meetings and at times I sit there in silence when others would feel the need to fill the void with talking. The silence doesn't bother me at all. And it allows the other person to talk freely and when there is that silence there, I am surprised at the depth of what some people will say when you allow them to do so. I've actually stepped on peoples feet in a meeting where they needed to shut up and listen because some key pieces of information were about to come forth. And it did. I've had people kick me on sales calls because it seemed like I was being passive and didn't know how to detect signs that someone was ready to buy. Yet I waited, and then, they tell me the last reason they are not yet ready to buy from me as if in a whisper. Now I've got the information I need to close the deal and everyone wins.

I have been on sales calls with high ranking executives that don't know how to shut up in those silent times. **I listen because I realize that in business meetings and in life, it's about them.** I had to make a very difficult call to an executive once and I got some coaching from my superior. He gave me a framework of the situation, gave me some suggestions and then said, *"say what you have to say, stand by it, and know when to shut up."* That was great insight. Sometimes when people get into uncomfortable situations they react funny. Some giggle uncontrollably, some clam up, some ramble. Having this insight helped me navigate through an ambush and I was able to find out what their concerns were and make my case. My points were solid and I had to make myself shut up a few times. But when I did, it made my points more solid, instead of trying to justify them and over explain them.

When we make conversations about the other person and not us, the floodgates will open up to us and we will be able to ascertain a wealth of information about them. Steer the conversation toward their interests; dig a little when you uncover something that may be of interest to them.

A number of years ago I was flown in to conduct a series of sales meetings. I was to meet with a total of 3 different executives who all had very different roles and backgrounds. I did my homework on the company, the market and the individual personalities. One was highly educated and cerebral, but didn't have the hands on experience that I had in the professional realm. Then next one did and was a lot like me. The final person was the highest ranking executive, who basically made the call, was sort of an entrepreneur, mild risk taker who really weighed his decisions carefully, a little nerdy, and was very proud of his accomplishments. My strategy with the last executive was to just let him talk. Let him ramble as much as possible. I had a series of questions that I had memorized that were relative to his accomplishments and interests. The questions I developed were centered on his motivation to pursue his dreams and his entrepreneurial spirit. When I was escorted into his office, I found it rather large, nicely decorated with quality furniture; a wonderful view of the skyline, and lots of personal memorabilia plastered on the walls. It was like a living testimony of his achievements. There were many pictures of him with celebrities and athletes. I'm sure some people got into his office (which could be both impressive and intimidating), looked around and asked questions about pictures of events, awards, trophies, his children's pictures that were everywhere. Not me, I stayed on task, asked the questions that I had planned, and sat back and listened. As the conversation progressed it was very conversational and flowed nicely. After an hour and a half, I left the meeting knowing that he felt really good about me because he got to talk about himself and I learned a lot about someone who developed himself and followed his dreams. Oh, and I got the contract.

CHALLENGE:

FOR YOUR NEXT MEETING, PREPARE A SERIES OF QUESTIONS THAT REQUIRE SOME THOUGHT AND WILL GET TO THE HEART OF THE ISSUE YOU ARE MEETING ABOUT. THESE QUESTIONS SHOULD PROVE THOUGHT AND ENGAGE THE OTHER PERSON.

I think the thing that differentiated me in that situation was that I asked quality questions that were different from others who would see an award or something in his office and manufacture interest when seeing a photo or award that caught their eye.

In other words, a lot of people ask about the same thing and I wanted to ask about something different. One, to distinguish myself and two, I am interested in what motivates people. The end result was that he went on and on, I asked a few follow up questions and basically directed the conversation. You may say that it sounds manipulative, but it's really not. Truth be told, he wasn't really interested in what I had to say. He likes to talk about himself. I've had subsequent interactions with him and I got sucked into thinking he really wanted to hear what I thought about his business since he was paying me as a consultant. Most of the time when I spoke to him or in his presence, he cut me off, vaguely disagreed and went back to his dissertation. After a couple of these interactions I didn't fall for the idea that he was interested in what I had to say. One time I thought to myself, "oh yeah, I forgot, he doesn't really want to hear what I have to say." I didn't take it personally, it's just the way he is and he has been successful in his own right, so I just had to let him talk because I'm not going to change the way he is.

Not everyone is like him. In fact, there are people who like to be able to converse back and forth enjoying an exchange of ideas. Some like to "inform or be informed." There should be joy in getting to know someone else and gaining from their experience and vantage point. And there is value in what someone else has to offer, even if you disagree.

A common mistake is to assume people think the same way. When in fact no two people are exactly the same and no two people should be treated the same way. Just because someone has a similar position, background, skill set, doesn't mean that they are the alike.

A few years later I met with another executive who had a similar background. I assumed that he too would be prone to talking about himself. He was smart, came from humble beginnings, and eventually developed an innovative and cutting edge product set with mass appeal. Prior to my meeting with him I did a little research and thought he was similar to the executive I spoke of previously. So I approached it in a similar way. I could tell he wanted me to ask him questions that stroked his ego, so I did. Then, BAM! The discussion became squarely focused on me and my background. I was caught off guard and found myself struggling to stay afloat as the barrage of questions came my way. He was asking the same type of questions I had been asking him – questions about my motivation, drive, background, what my qualifications were, what my weaknesses were, how I matched up with the direction of his empire. In a few short minutes he exposed my weakness and then asked about my watch (which was much more expensive than his) He asked to see it so I took it off and showed him proudly. Only people who know about watches would recognize mine, but he did and he admired it.

After I left his office, which was also impressive, it was obvious to me that I was unprepared to talk about myself when asked, then I got flattered when he admired my watch and I allowed the focus to become on me, which is what he wanted. The second I walked out of his office, I knew I wasn't going to get the deal. It was one of those rare occasions where I got filleted, and the master taught me a lesson. I made the mistake of thinking I could steer the conversation toward him, which he allowed for a bit, but then I found myself in his crosshairs and was not prepared.

KEY POINT:

NO TWO PEOPLE ARE EXACTLY ALIKE, SO DON'T TREAT THEM AS IF THEY ARE. EACH INDIVIDUAL WILL HAVE DIFFERENT TRAITS AND HABITS, SO IDENTIFY THEM AND HANDLE THEM AS A UNIQUE INDIVIDUAL.

You cannot assume that just because people are similar, that they are alike. If you do you will fail to make the connection with others because you are, AGAIN, prejudging them. That puts people in a box, and you wouldn't want to be put in a box, would you?

Hopefully it is apparent that any time you are with another individual it is not an opportunity to brag about yourself or flaunt your ego (I believe in letting others do that), but a chance to communicate with another person and add to their life or gain from their experience, whether good or bad.

2

About You

Let's talk about your favorite subject…YOU! You really do have something unique to give to others, no question. You are a sum total of your experiences in life. Your perspective is one of a kind and there is no one quite like you. Each of us can add or detract from a conversation depending on what you put into it. So, what do you want people to say about you? How do you want people to perceive you? Do you want people to like you? What do you think of yourself?

These are all things we have control of. Not each individual aspect, but we can influence how we are perceived by building a good reputation. Under NO circumstances should we paint a picture that is false or inflated. You should be yourself and be true to who you are. There are things you can bring to a conversation or dialogue that can be beneficial. Believe that and try and identify what you have to offer so you are aware of it. For example, your hobbies may not be fascinating to everyone, but what is it about your interests that others would be able to relate to? Just because someone may not like golf, doesn't mean that they can't relate to your effort, humor, or enjoyment of the game.

So what is your role in conversation? Glad you asked. Going back to Ben Franklin's quote, "to inform or to be informed". This is an excellent rule of thumb and what a great guide it can be in our conversations. So, stop and mentally ask yourself in a conversation, *am I informing or being informed*? That is a great way to keep ourselves honest and on point. Now, sometimes I like to clown around in conversation and that's ok too. But to really get to the depth of who you are and to truly have a discourse, we need to open up and talk WITH the other person.

CHALLENGE:

THE NEXT TIME YOU ARE IN A CONVERSATION, STOP AND ASK YOURSELF, "AM I BEING INFORMED, OR AM I INFORMING?"

So, how would you rate yourself in this category on a scale of 1 to 10? What are your conversations like? Are they generally negative or positive? Are they about you and what you do or are they about them? Do people seek out your advice or do they run when they see you coming?

What do you remember the next time you see them? Do you forget what was said or do you recall details?

A huge aspect in conversation is being able to recollect what was said and listening to what the other person says. How many times have you been to an electronics store and asked about a particular item and the sales clerk brings you over to something more expensive and beyond what you asked for. Then you re-clarify what you wanted to look at, and they take you to see items that would fit the bill, but then you walk back over to the item that he pointed out. Well, he's trying to make a sale and many times it will be effective because, you set a budget for an item, but may be willing to expand your budget because it really wows you. You may not need it, but you can't say NO because you feel you should have it.

The problem is that the salesperson isn't listening to you and you are allowing someone else to influence the outcome of the interaction. Because in this situation it was about me and not him. Sometimes we allow it to be about us and not them, why? Because by nature we are self-centered and concerned about our own wants. People generally don't see the big picture and realize that by getting the focus off yourself, you will also get what you want.

I have had a long career as a professional salesman and something that has really helped me is listening to people and giving them what they want. Sounds simplistic, doesn't it? You can only do this by listening and not focusing on yourself. I have been in meetings where a salesperson was asking questions about the customer and was only looking for a way to sell them what **HE** was thinking he could sell them. Its not about what you think you can sell them either. The artful process of conversation in a sales situation isn't about what YOU think YOU can sell them, or what YOU think YOU can get away with selling them. When you think that way, you will never have satisfied customers in the long run because you are not connecting the dots as to what they really need. In the end, this will be a dissatisfied customer or strained friendship.

Once at a car dealership I was negotiating the purchase of a vehicle. I found the one I wanted on the lot, drove it and decided to make the purchase. I looked at the sticker price in the window and told the salesman that my payments needed to be so much and my down payment would be so much and the term should be such and such. So about 20 minutes later he came back with an outrageous figure scribbled on a piece of paper which was almost double what I told him I wanted to pay. I took the piece of paper, carefully examined it, and asked if this was the best he could do. He responded with a definitive yes. So I took the sheet of paper, crumbled it up and threw it across the room and told him to get back in there with his manager and try a lot harder or I'm leaving. If I'm honest, I was a little irritated because he was not only trying to rip me off, but totally ignored what I specifically laid out for him. Prior to that I had no reason not to trust him, but after that I only saw him as a cheap salesman who was trying to take advantage of me. I eventually walked off the lot in disgust.

When people focus on themselves, the results are predictable and unfavorable. Focusing on yourself will not satisfy everyone involved. Sure, we should have in mind what we want to get in a given situation. But as the famous motivational speaker Zig Ziglar has said many, many times, "You will get what you want, if you help enough other people get what they want."

Ah, so we should focus on what other people want? **YES**! Quite right my good fellow. So many times in business transactions, I am more concerned about helping others than helping myself. That's because I really like helping people and I know that when I help someone I will get something in return – <u>my first and dominant motive is to help others</u>.

Challenge:

When in a conversation, take a step back and ask yourself, "What do <u>they</u> *REALLY* want?" And DON'T assume.

To that point; I NEVER expect something in return from them nor do I think that they owe me something. This is because I believe in a law that is: **when you give, you will receive**. Now I did say that when I help someone else, I will receive a benefit – YES I DID! But I have found that many times I do pick up extra business or get a contract that I didn't expect from an unknown referral or a bonus from out of the blue. This has happened to me more times than I can count.

    Once I was working on a sales team and I was really trying to hit my numbers toward the end of the fiscal year. I found myself in unusual territory, I was WAY behind my numbers with only a few days to go and it looked like I was going to fall far short of my goals. This really bothered me and I wasn't going to go down without a fight. For those few days I worked even harder than I had previously, focusing on the best activities that would help me exceed my goal. Now, I knew that some other salespeople were taking short cuts, overselling, using questionable methods, and in my opinion, they would pay for it in the near future. Admittedly, I was tempted to take a short cut and enjoy the short lived recognition, only to reap the consequences in the future. But I held fast to my conviction and focused on doing the right thing by my customers. There were times that I could have compromised, but I didn't. The day after the fiscal year ended, I was driving to work and I was thinking about how I was unhappy that I didn't exceed my goal and fell short. I was in a funny mood and I wasn't used to not being a total success. But as I was going into the office, I thought to myself, "Oh well, at least I did it the right way and I did my best – but if there is any way for something miraculous, something really amazing, some way to still be victorious, show me the way." When I got to my desk, the red light was blinking on my phone, meaning I had a message, and it was a customer that I had left about a dozen messages with. They apologized for not getting back to me any sooner and that they really needed my help and basically begged me to meet with them that day. I checked with my boss and he agreed that if I were to get signed contracts that day; he would allow the sale to go through. In short, I was a mile from my quota and my team had fallen short as well. That sale got me over 100%, got my team over plan and I won a trip too.

Luck? I think not. To quote Thomas Jefferson, *"I'm a great believer in luck, and I find the harder I work the more I have of it."*

If I had focused on myself and been short sighted, I may have had temporary success, but no long term success, nor the joy of knowing that I did it the right way and with integrity. I am proud of my accomplishments during that time and I believe that because I had the right focus and attitude, that my success was inevitable.

When you focus your attention on others instead of yourself, you will be amazed how much you are able to connect with others and pick up on the subtle nuances of their personality and character. You can understand what drives them, why they keep moving on, the challenges they have had and how they persevered amidst great adversity. There is also a great chance to gain something for yourself and to learn something that maybe only they can teach you. In a business environment this can give you a huge advantage. When you know what the other wants, it makes your life a lot easier and can save you a lot of trouble.

Focusing on the other person instead of YOU, will help you get what YOU ultimately want. Charitable giving in our country is something many people participate in. I can't tell you how many United Way presentations I have sat through and all the unrealistic statistics they utilize to present their case for you giving them money. I'm not opposed to making a case for giving and showing how the money is utilized, but don't insult my intelligence by inflating the facts.

I give a lot of money to a few select charities that I believe in and do it because I want to see them succeed in their mission. No one needs to pressure me into anything like that. Personally, I give more money to charity than a lot of high ranking political officials. The reason I do it is because I enjoy giving. Some give so they can brag about how much they give, but I believe that's the wrong motive for giving. It does feel good knowing that I give, but I give because I choose to do so, not because anyone forces me to.

The other thing about charities is that almost all of them have so much overhead that only a small portion of the money actually gets to where it is supposed to go. In most cases more money goes to administration than to the actual purpose of the charity. So I am a bit leery of charities. Now, they're not all bad, but just because they are a 501c3 does not mean they are operating above board. Its just that if you are giving out of your pocket, you should know what you are actually giving to. People give because they want to share out of what they have been blessed with, and that's a great motive and wonderful way to get the focus off of yourself.

To put things in context, YOU matter and are important. But in interactions with others, don't dominate the conversation by talking about yourself. Open it up a little and give others a chance to get involved and gear the subject to them. Concentrate on what YOU have to give and how you can help others.

CHALLENGE:

GIVING – WHEN IN CONVERSATIONS, WHAT ARE YOU GIVING AND CONTRIBUTING? TEST YOURSELF ON THIS AND BE HONEST ABOUT YOUR EFFECT ON THE CONVERSATION.

When I used to visit my grandfather one thing I enjoyed was listening to him talk about his life and the wisdom with which he spoke. He was one of the most honest men I have ever known and it was great to be able to spend time with him and expose my children to him. During those visits I would take a back seat and take it all in. I tried to draw things out of him and connect with him. We loved talking about hockey and other sports. From him

I learned a lot about my heritage, in which he had a lot of pride. Those trips to see him were priceless and I only wish that I had the opportunity to spend more time with him.

Once, we were at dinner and my daughter kept putting silverware in his pocket without him knowing it and then we would accuse him of trying to steal the silverware. We all had a big laugh out of that and thoroughly enjoyed being together. You cannot replace someone like that in your life and once they are gone, they are gone. So make the moments of your life count and seize the day.

Realize what makes you who you are and keep all of that in perspective as you interact in your daily routine. You are important and have the ability to add value, so do it when appropriate.

Focusing on what's important to others may be a foreign concept or it may not, but unless you have perfected the art of focusing on others and understanding them, then put these practical tips into action.

3

Negotiating

Any time we are in the presence of another individual, there is some form of negotiating going on. In conversation we endeavor to communicate our ideals, sell concepts, and win someone over. So, do you think you can win them over by bragging about you, or your kids, or your fancy car, NO! I'd throw you out of my house if you talk like that around me. The truth is in negotiating most people are focused on what they feel they should get and not the other person.

Several years ago I was working with an entrepreneur on some concepts to grow his market share and protect his customers. I was under some rigid guidelines that were making it difficult for me to do business with him. Previously several other salespeople attempted to win his business (which was significant). During the negotiating process he was very particular about how he felt the deal should be structured. So, rather than just say, yes or no to his terms, I began digging a little into why he felt the way he did. Boy, did I learn a lot about his business and industry. He basically was asking for a more lengthy payout structure than normal because of the overhead and upfront cost in completing the transaction. Once I understood where he was coming from and the reasons he wanted it this way I had more conviction in upholding my end because I was able to relate to where he was coming from. We wound up doing not only that transaction, but several more afterward.

CHALLENGE:

IMPASSE – WHEN YOU REACH AN IMPASSE, DON'T SHUT DOWN AND GIVE UP. FIND OUT WHAT THE ROAD BLOCK IS AND WHY IT'S THERE. ASK THE HARD QUESTIONS LIKE, "WHY DOES THIS NOT MAKE SENSE TO YOU?"

Sometimes it's difficult to earn the business, but because of the extra effort involved those can be some of the most rewarding and long lasting business relationships.

When my daughter was about 4 years old, my mom was visiting and we were at an outdoor shopping area that was packed with a variety of trendy stores and restaurants. We had just left a restaurant and I was walking with my mom and my daughter. As we passed an ice cream shop my daughter began talking about how much she loved ice cream. She was smiling, batting her eyes at me and going on and on about how she would really love to have some ice cream from the shop we just passed. She wouldn't let up either. Now she managed to do this without being annoying or whining. Honestly, it was difficult to resist. I have a soft spot for my daughter, so I didn't see any reason to stand between her and her happiness. When I told her that I would buy her the ice cream, she got all excited and told me I was the best daddy in the whole world. That felt good to me. Then my mom says, "Boy she sure has you wrapped around her finger." She's right. Had I said NO to the ice cream she probably would not have said that I was the best daddy in the entire world, but since I did say yes, now I was. HHMMMMM, interesting.

A couple of things she did right. One, she didn't ask in an annoying or obnoxious way. Two, she knew she could play on my emotions, mainly my love for her. Three, she struck the balance between persistent and pushy. Four, she followed it with a compliment which was unparalleled and which reinforced that I had made the right decision. So basically, she sold me and negotiated what she wanted. But do you know what? So did I. I got the pleasure of making my daughter happy and watching her enjoy that ice cream. It was worth every penny I spent on it.

To my daughter, she didn't know that I got what I wanted, she was just happy to be able to eat ice cream.

When you think of negotiating, what comes to mind? Attorneys, lots of litigation, arguing, etc. Negotiating is not about holding out for what you want and trying to take advantage of the other person.

I was in a competitive situation once with another salesman whom I knew of (by reputation and a good one at that) in which we managed the same account. The owner was a great guy and I developed a wonderful rapport with him over the years. One particular year the business owner was unhappy with the amount of money he was spending (2/3 on my product) and decided to take 100% of his budget and spend it with my competitor. He shared that it was nothing personal, but he felt he could reduce his expenditure and get an even better product from the competitor. **What would you have done**? Truthfully, both products were necessary to maintain the flow of his business and if he were to do without mine, it would hurt him. When I learned this several months later, I thought to myself what I would have done if presented with that opportunity. Maybe I would have said, yeah, you don't need them anyway, I'll get you an upgrade and it will be great for both of us. I know my superiors would have applauded my efforts. Anyway, my competitor said, "Look, you can't do that, cancelling the other product will ultimately hurt you, this is unethical and I won't be a part of it." After I picked my jaw off of the floor, I thought about how upright and honest my competitor was. I also know how much more respect my customer had for him too. You never gain anything by bashing competitors. It's always better to take the high road. Many times the road less traveled.

In negotiations, always be aware of what the other person wants and try to accommodate. True negotiation is not a winner take all, except in extreme situations where someone is obviously trying to take advantage of someone's wealth or trying to hurt someone.

With this mind-set, you are more free to work on a win/win strategy. You see this in politics, where both sides dig in and refuse to budge and nothing ever gets done – THEY ARE NOT FOCUSING ON WHO THEY ARE SUPPOSED TO REPRESENT. You also see times when there is an obvious agenda, and that's not right either because they are not truly doing the job they were elected to do, but focusing on a side benefit for themselves or someone else.

Also in negotiations, DO NOT assume you really know what the other person wants. Ask questions, second and third level questions to understand what it is that they want. They may be asking for money, but what they really want is to be recognized for something they did. **What they ask for and what they want *may not* be the same thing**. I said that they MAY NOT be the same, but sometimes they may be. So it's your job to be clear on the difference. So sometimes, they are asking for compensation, and are expecting it too.

One thing that can help negotiations is letting the other person know that you are concerned about them and how the outcome will impact them. There was a business I was considering buying. It had been established for a long time and had a great reputation for good service. Some of the assets were trucks, storage space, a little land, and employees. As I was in negotiations with the owners, I was evaluating the value of the company and was prepared to pay them a percentage of the value of the revenue for a 3 year period, plus assets. After pouring over the numbers for several days I had a figure in mind, but felt it was unfair to them, so I sat down with them and told them how I felt and that I believed that the real number of the business was a figure they wouldn't be able to live with. I apologized for taking up their time and thanked them for their cooperation. What they told me was they wanted to get some value for their business, but they also wanted the legacy of the family business to succeed. But the gap between what they wanted and what it was truly worth was too great.

Sometimes it's difficult to work with someone because they may be a bit closed off or even hostile. It is more challenging to get to a win/win in situations like that. In my experience you need to be professional, polite and not react to anger, insults, or threats.

One difficult account I managed was a beauty salon. As I was servicing the account for the first time I discovered they had been overpromised as to the performance of a product. What they actually got was far from their lofty expectations they had been promised. To that point I had made numerous attempts to meet them and handle the situation, but no response. So I sent a certified letter after months of attempts to reach them. The first conversation I had with the owner was not pleasant. He was condescending, haughty about his position, and generally unpleasant. Now, I'm not one to be easily offended because I don't take that type of whining personal, so I just let him get it all out and apologized for his previous experience. I even tried to get him going again a few times – ensuring he had completely vented all of his frustration. He further tried to tell me about how great his business was and that he didn't need my marketing tools to generate new business. He bragged about his client retention rate and how he retained 75% of his clients and no other competitor was able to match that. BAM! I had the ammunition I needed to make my point. This was my field of expertise and he should just leave that to me and I won't tell him how to cut hair. So I said, "75% huh?" he said, "yes and that is excellent, and that's why I don't need your services any longer." I replied, "Well, some salons I talk to have a 90% retention rate, just saying." He was silent. My final word was this, "So every year you lose 25% of your customers, and you think you can run a business without replacing the customers you lose. In 4 years you will have lost all your customers and I believe in doing so you could jeopardize your business – is that what you want?" He grudgingly said that he appreciated my input but that I really didn't know what I was talking about. A few weeks later my manager came to me and showed me a letter from that business owner complaining about my "tactics" and that he should fire me because I endeavored to overturn his decision to discontinue our services. I explained the situation to him and told him exactly what I had said and we moved on. About 4 months later I called the business back to see how they were doing and to see if they had a change of heart. THEY DID! They were out of business, just as I told them they would. Now, I'm not rejoicing in this at all because they could have avoided going out of business. But in these particular negotiations, the other party allowed emotions rather than level headed thinking to dominate their logic. In the end they made a critical error in the direction of their business and it cost them everything.

Challenge:

The next time you are in the midst of negotiations, get clarity on what they want to get out of the situation. Put on their shoes for a bit to gain perspective on why they feel the way they do.

A great rule in negotiating. DON'T ALLOW EMOTIONS TO RULE YOUR LOGIC IN NEGOTIATIONS. You have got to be cool, and like I said, focus on what they want in negotiations. It will really pay off.

So, in negotiating, you have to understand what the other party wants, as well as what you want. It doesn't have to be a knockdown, drag-out affair. It can be done, not only in a civil manner, but it is usually possible for everyone to win. So focus on them and what they want. This will give you a better understanding of what you are facing and where you stand.

4

About Goals

When we have goals that are realistic, concrete and written down, we have the potential to achieve and exceed our expectations. When we don't, we will be like most people that just float along and get what comes their way. IF YOU ARE INTERESTED IN SUCCESS, THEN YOU **MUST** HAVE WRITTEN GOALS. After talking with and interviewing hundreds of top performers around the country, one of the things they have in common is that they have concrete goals that they are committed to achieving. Something else is that they usually have a reason or purpose for the attainment of that plateau. Many times its recognition, or a promotion, or a bonus, or a number of other motivating factors.

Many financial goals are set in light of children going to college, retirement, taking care of family members, taking someone on a trip, buying that vacation home, buying a better house, home improvement, hobbies, visiting old friends across the country, to mention a few. In most cases these will involve other people, which is not a selfish motive when you consider that no one desires riches to sit alone by them self on a pile of gold and not share it with anyone. Human beings by nature want to be in the presence of other humans.

So why is this significant? I'm glad you asked! It's very relevant in two ways. One, we want to share it with someone and have the desire to be recognized by others. Two, in order to attain those goals; we must offer some type of service, or product, that is truly beneficial to someone else. If we don't, then our labor is something we cannot be proud of and we will not be able to sleep at night. The point is that we don't build success upon taking advantage of other people. There are no short cuts to genuine success. Success not built on solid principle will not last. Remember the dot.com bust. Many who see fortunes come quickly also see them go quickly too. Not saying that you can't accumulate wealth in a relatively short time, but it must be done the right way. But you never gain anything significant at the expense of someone else.

By the right way, I mean that your business is to be conducted in an honest, open and ethical manner. No sleight of hand here. I've seen some who succumb to the notion that wealth can be quickly gained if you cheat, or do not fully disclose details. They may experience short lived gain, but they will not have long lasting success. It's because they violated a principle.

In the bible it says, "A good name is rather to be chosen than great riches." Is it really success if you compromise your integrity? Yet how easily some give it away. The manner in which we conduct ourselves and our business is important.

CHALLENGE:

GOALS – IF YOU HAVE NOT WRITTEN DOWN ANY GOALS, THEN START NOW. WRITE DOWN SOME SHORT TERM AND SOME LONG TERM GOALS. INCLUDE A TIMELINE, PURPOSE AND FIGURE IN WHAT IT WILL TAKE TO ACHIEVE YOUR GOAL.

One thing about goals is that if you build a company, product, device, service or whatever, with the idea of how it will benefit people, you will have a better chance for success than if you simply do it with the idea of making money. So if we begin with the end in mind, we can build something we can be proud of. This is true of a business, friendship, hobby, etc.

Think of the innovations of Apple. Their financial success is undeniable and one major factor is that they make products that people want. They don't start with the attitude of just making money from customers without giving something in return. They seek to be innovative and they recognize that if they focus on what the customers want, they will eventually reach the financial goals they have. And they have proven this time and time again.

The old adage, "Greed is good", is not a creed you can live by and build success upon. We build by keeping others in mind when setting and achieving goals. We don't say, "how many of these do I have to sell to make a million dollars?" We should say, "How many people can I help with what I have to offer." Much better huh?

To be clear, we begin with the end in mind and envision how our product or service will benefit people. An excellent question to ask ourselves would be, "What is this really going to do for people"? When we begin there, the outcome has a much better chance for being successful.

When I owned a construction company I had goals and a vision of success. But one thing I knew is that, if I provided better workmanship and a fair price, I would be successful and exceed my goals for the business. Making money was a byproduct of the way I ran my business and took care of the customer. There were times that I broke even or lost money on a job. That was ok because I felt I needed to satisfy the customer, which I did. In times like that, when the job was finished, I felt good about how I made it right. In the future I didn't have to worry about a bad reputation because my goal was to keep my customer happy. I was proud of that venture because I did it my way and I had the chance to practice the principles I knew were true. I got a ton of referrals as well because I made sure the work was done correctly.

My phone rang one hectic day and it was a customer complaining about a defect in my work and demanded that I fix it. I assured her that we would come and take care of it. I pulled my top foreman off a job so he could fix it personally. Afterward I was told that they liked dealing with me because I came highly recommended and I lived up to the reputation.

On another occasion I was having trouble with a subcontractor completing some detail on a job, for which they had already been paid (note to self, NEVER pay a subcontractor fully until the job is completed no matter what his sob story is). Anyway I kept assuring the customer that we would complete the detail work we promised. I kept trying to get in contact with the sub to no avail. This went on for several weeks and the customer was kind but I could tell their patience was running thin. My sign was in their yard and the work wasn't finished. This looked bad on me. So I finally broke down and hired another sub to finish the trim work to complete the job. I came back when it was all done and met with the homeowners. The look on their faces was worth everything. The house now looked like one of the best on the block, it looked really fantastic. I broke even on that job, but it was really satisfying because I made an elderly couple happy with their home. My first goal in that job was to please the customer, and that's what I did. The payoff was to come later by way of the referrals because my sign was in their yard

That mindset can be applied in any situation. If you are concerned about the other person, it's almost like you mysteriously are taken care of. However, it seems that it's human nature to fend for themselves and to be wary of others raiding their pot of gold.

While working on a particular sales team there seemed to be endless overlapping territories and constant bickering from simple minded people who were concerned, not about doing the right thing, but doing whatever it takes to make sales even if it meant sacrificing ethical standards. Confusion and contention was the norm. In speaking to management they weren't interested in doing the right thing as much as they were maximizing their numbers and profits. This was very frustrating for me because I was trying to do the right thing and it was difficult in that environment. The atmosphere was sort of like a cancer. Everyone was out for themselves, suspicion ran rampant, some were jealous of others, gossip flew like the wind, and favoritism was prevalent. Even those who were successful were not happy and it was no fun working in that environment.

When selfish motives prevail, not much good comes out of it. In fact it brings out the worst in people. After a while, I'd had enough and moved on. And guess what? It changed my life. I didn't have to deal with the overbearingly negative attitudes of people who were self-indulged in their own egos and I found it quite refreshing. If you are in an atmosphere where you are surrounded by negative people with small minds, my advice to you is to MOVE ON! Leave them in the dust. Don't wish evil on them, just leave them behind and look forward.

Challenge:

Are there people in your life that drag you down and suck the life out of you? Negativity people are counter-productive. Either help them to be positive or disassociate yourself from them.

I lived in a dorm once and there was someone that lived a few doors down who had a strange habit. They used to walk out the door and walk toward my room, yet their head was turned looking in the other direction. A few times

I almost bumped into them and finally one day I did. A little annoyed I said, "Ya know, your eyes and feet are pointed in the same direction." In other words, move in the same direction as your feet. When you move in a direction, focus on where you are going, not where you've been.

I was in a band a few years back and one of my close friends in the band was moving. We did a lot of things together and had a great friendship. When we were saying our goodbyes, he told me; "Hey, when I move on, I move on. I'll stay in touch, but I'm not going to call you every day." To be honest, I was taken back at first because of all we had been through. But I thought about it and I knew he was right. When you move geographically, your sphere of influence is different and you make new friends and acquaintances.

There may be things that keep you from achieving your goals, so get rid of them. In order to move in the direction of your goals, you must eliminate distractions. Whether it's changing jobs, or things that are not congruent with your goals, if it doesn't add to you, then purge it.

One thing, as it relates to goals, is that we like to be recognized for our efforts in the presence of our peers, those with whom we work and labor alongside. Most companies have award banquets and trips for those who perform and exceed expectations. People generally like to be recognized for their efforts in front of peers. I can't tell you how many times I have received positive recognition for my accomplishments and it gives me a sense of accomplishment and pride. An offshoot of that is a lot more confidence and belief in myself. There is something to be said for public recognition that affirms your achievements. It has little to do with ego and a lot to do with pride in making your mark – hitting goals and your ability to perform at a high level.

5

Conversation

The definition of conversation is: "*The informal exchange of ideas by spoken words*." Every day, unless we are a hermit, we have the privilege of conversing with other people.

One of my first jobs was a telemarketing sales rep. My job was to make outbound calls, talking to decision makers and selling advertising space. Once the correct person would get on the phone I would give them my "pitch" - read from a script and delivered with force and passion. After a period of time I became successful and honed my skills. I got to be one of the elite salesmen in my field. I surpassed many older and more experienced representatives in sales volume. After I learned the basics, I added my own style and then it became natural to me.

One thing I didn't do then, which I have learned since, is to have more of a dialogue, a conversation. Like I said in the first chapter, I was talking AT people and not with them. Asking questions or provoking thought is what draws people in and then you engage in a two way dialogue. There is an art of conversation. I was missing the boat.

For some, conversation comes easily, for me it did not. I used to stutter, sometimes could hardly get some words out. It wasn't every word or phrase, but when I got excited, or afraid, I would stutter and then it would get worse.

I think one thing that helped me was to get a job in sales. For one, I had to talk for a living and convince them to buy something they weren't anticipating buying and buying on the spot. It helped me get over stuttering.

However, the "pitch", as it was called, was a script that I memorized and was designed to take turns depending on the response. In effect, this was a manufactured conversation. It wasn't real. And it wasn't about them; it was about what I wanted.

One thing I learned from this experience was how to structure a sales pitch. There had to be an introduction, an opening, the main body, a trust checker or validation, strong reason why they need to do this now, and a very strong closing question. From this I've developed trainings for individuals and companies that can help improve the efficiency of their sales efforts and appointment setting. It has also helped me over the years set appointments for myself.

Since then, I further incorporated something else. Interaction. That is something I was missing. And I do not mean a manufactured interaction, as it has become so natural that I just start talking and get a conversation going naturally.

People will open up to your human side when you show compassion and vulnerability. What I mean by that is this: If you show that you need someone's help, they are usually more willing to help you than if you demand they do something for you. I cannot tell you how many times I have been in an office and I didn't know the name of the person that would be able to help me. So I would walk in and say, *"Hi, how are you, I'm Todd with XYZ company and I was hoping to speak to the person who does such and such."* And my tone was light, friendly and soft. Some people that know me have seen me do this and are surprised that I use that tone. The reason I do, is that I genuinely need their help, and they could either help me or could make it difficult for me.

That brings me to my next point here – tone. The tone in which you speak is a key factor in how people receive your message.

When I was younger I was more like a bull in a china shop. My manner was more forceful in my conversations which could be misunderstood for being harsh and direct. Many times my normal tone was strong and confident. One thing I had was confidence and I was passionate about what I believed. When people disagreed with me I didn't back down easily and when I was on sales calls, let's just say I didn't take no for an answer and was accustomed to getting my way.

I had a job selling real estate in which I had to get prospects interested and get them to meet with me. Of all the people there, I stood out as a leader and top performer.

The company had a new line of properties that I wanted to be a part of and I wanted to sell them so I spoke to the owner and told him that I wanted to be on that project. In my mind, I fully expected to have my way. He flat out told me NO. Angrily, I gave him 4 or 5 more reasons that I SHOULD be on that team. He said no again. By this time I was insistent and intensified my tone and demanded that allow me to sell those properties or I would quit. He refused, I told him he was dead wrong, he didn't know how to run his business and walked out. We were both angry when I left and everyone in the office heard the argument. People generally didn't stand up to the owner because he was a brash individual who intimidated most people who worked for him. When I walked out of his office, which had paper thin walls, everyone was frozen still with their jaws open and watched me walk out.

No matter how hard I tried to hammer my point home, my idea was rejected. Truthfully I was surprised when he didn't give in. I was used to getting my way in situations like that and I would have been successful in that endeavor.

Then I was shocked when he didn't call me and beg me to come back to work for him. But after a few days I called him because I missed working there. When I got the owner on the phone we talked and he told me that he was put in a difficult position. He could not give into me because he felt he would lose control and appear weak. This surprised me. I finally got where he was coming from. He was used to ruling the office with an iron fist. Working there for a few months, I understood how he operated; I just wasn't intimidated by him.

A couple of things I learned from that situation. First, I just tried to make my case, and then restated it more forcefully each time, to the point of yelling. I didn't listen to him or even ask him about why he didn't see things my way. Second, the more I turned up the heat, the more he shut down and got angry. Third, I didn't consider the impact my tone would have on others around us. He didn't come right out and tell me he'd lose power if he gave in to me (others did that), but it was clear after our conversation subsequent to the argument. Fourth, I should have considered the setting as well. When you are in someone else's office, they have home field advantage. It would be like someone coming to your house and letting their dog go to the bathroom on your lawn in front of you, not clean it up and smile after it happened. Fifth, I learned that I could not always hammer my way through any given situation.

Challenge:

The next time you are in a difficult conversation, consider your tone and how it is impacting the conversation. Mark how it affects the dialogue.

Our tone is vitally important in conversation. The way you say things will affect how people react to you. When you watch people sing a song, be aware of how they present themselves as they perform. If it's a sad song, their facial expressions should reflect it as well as the vocal tone. If it's energetic and uplifting, the same should apply.

There is more than one way to communicate and we should be aware of it. When I talk to certain people, I am aware if they are mild mannered and try to be aware of that when speaking to them. Some are bold as brass, so they should be handled accordingly – not that you are mean, but direct and to the point.

Conversation is a bi-directional discourse and your tone and attitude should set the table for the exchange of thoughts. As I said earlier, many people used to interpret my tone as arrogance and cockiness, so they would treat me that way. People will label you. I was having lunch with a group of people and there was a woman there who did editing and proof reading. We began to talk about her approach and her life. I asked questions about books and writers and styles and classic literature during the conversation. Most of the conversation was about her and her work because I was interested in it. This individual was very much an introvert, the opposite of me, so I decided to have a little fun and ask about how her experience translates into social situations. I asked her if she felt you can judge a book by its cover, meaning that you can look at someone and know all about them, to which she replied emphatically "yes." I said, "*Really, so you are saying that you can tell about someone just by their appearance?*" She again replied, "yes." I came right out and said, "*No you can't and I think it is a little judgmental to have that point of view. You can't judge a book by its cover*." She said, "*sometimes you can*." So I asked her if she can tell about me by looking at me, even though she had the benefit of knowing a little about me. She agreed. Specifically I asked her if she thought she could tell about the music I liked, hobbies, interests, background, work history, education, and what motivates me. She responded in the positive and proceeded. WOW, DEAD WRONG ON ALL POINTS! As my respect for her greatly diminished I asked her how she could be so sure she is right, when she is totally off. She stumbled through some justification and said that **usually** you can judge a book by its cover. One interesting fact is that I pre-judged her as being socially inept and narrow minded. Hhmmmm.

CHALLENGE:

DON'T PRE-JUDGE OTHER PEOPLE. INSTEAD, ASK QUESTIONS AND GIVE THEM AN OPPORTUNITY TO REVEAL THEMSELVES TO YOU RATHER THAN ASSUMING.

I'm amazed at how we prejudge and stereotype people. If we are in a business or selling situation we had better not judge people or it will cost you. But the habit begins in our personal life in conversations with friends and family.

There are many factors that impact our conversations. We should take into account the other person and make sure they are engaged in stimulating conversation and be mindful of them in the discourse. Making conversation is an art and we should become the master of it. It pays off.

6

Listening

Now this should be an obvious component in a book titled "It's all about them…not you." And you would be right. Listening is almost a lost art in some cultures. It is a highly undervalued skill and most don't see the greatness of it.

It's a fact that we have two ears and one mouth, so we should listen twice as much as we talk, and that's a good rule of thumb. So here are some ways we can improve our listening skills and get more out of conversations by hearing what the other is saying.

Sometimes people are thinking about what they want to say as the other person is talking. I've been guilty of that more than I care to admit. I mentioned earlier that if you do that, you will miss key pieces of information that are vital in understanding the other person and their point.

When talking with another individual no matter what type of personality they have, it should never be a bore, instead try and find something in it for you.

I was on a road trip with another salesman driving several hours to an appointment and this individual was rambling about meaningless blather. I was annoyed before we buckled our seatbelts. After a half an hour or so it was obvious that I was annoyed and getting tired of it, and was no longer trying to hide it. However, the more I got annoyed, the more the other person would just ramble more and try and get me engaged by demanding a response to rhetorical questions (which don't require a response). I tried so hard to ignore them but I could not. Now I knew this person had a lot of experience and knowledge in the field, probably twice as much as I did and I couldn't figure out how to get out of the situation. Then it dawned on me to redirect the conversation. So I began asking about their experience with specific questions about how they handled difficult clients, gaining business, customer relations, closing business, and public speaking. I kept firing questions at him, directing the conversation toward what I wanted to talk about. After a bit, I was now engaged. But I didn't let down, I kept it up by asking second and third level questions, digging for answers. In all, we had a great trip and I learned a lot from him.

A good lesson here is to always try to get something from the conversation. When you make it about them and draw from their experience, you will be amazed at how much you can gain. Now I've been around the person since and am still annoyed by his personality traits, but learned to draw on his wisdom by focusing on him.

Another thing is to avoid becoming distracted by bad habits. There I was, in a national sales conference with over a thousand other sales professionals getting ready to hear the next speaker. As they introduced her, they played up her background, and her book. Then she came out and began speaking. Now one of my pet peeves is the filler phrase, "and um." She did it a few times and then I started marking down on my notepad every time she used it. It came up again and again – over and over. I was so distracted by that bad speaking habit that I literally did not hear a word she said. After it was over, I asked the person next to me what he thought, he replied, "it was ok, AND UM." He heard what I did. Filler phrases are a speech killer and can really distract audiences from being able to listen to you.

You should record yourself on sales calls, or talking with customers on the phone or maybe just practicing your sales presentation. You will really be surprised how you sound and if it's painful for you to listen to, imagine how painful it is for others to listen to you.

So, when you are listening, a good listener will tune out those distractions. And a good speaker will eliminate them from his speech. The same is true in a conversation where only two are involved.

In any conversation there is usually a central theme, especially in a business discussion. You need to be clear and stay on point. Direct and clarify the conversation by asking relevant questions that get to the real issues.

At that same sales conference the very next speaker had lived in New York City and was talking about how customers make buying decisions. This speaker had me at hello. He spoke for about an hour. His presentation flew by and he made some really great points. He didn't use any "filler-phrases" but was engaging, utilized multimedia, charts, quotes and graphs that all tied into his central theme.

I felt like he was talking right to me. At one point he showed a video that he made to enhance his point, which was how to affect the decision making process of a buyer, and more specifically how to catch their attention at that point and redirect them. For me it was really impactful and meaningful because it related to me. And even if it didn't, it was so interesting that I could have listened all day because of how he related to people

When we are listening, we should be clear on what the central theme is and stay on point at all times. And when we are clear on what the theme is, the illustrations and statistics will ring clear to us and have more meaning.

So how do you fare in conversations? Do you track where the conversation is going or do you stray off the path and redirect to suit your liking?

Challenge:

In your next conversation, stop and see if you can clearly identify the central theme of the discussion.

Sometimes we may have a tendency to get caught up on emotional words rather than look for their meaning in the context. Do not react to them; listen in terms of the flow of the conversation. Even if you don't like how it is used or said, grasp the idea and move on. Some get lost in a few phrases or colorful words and miss the point.

When people get worked up they may tend to describe things rather colorfully, as if painting a landscape picture. See the picture for what it is, rather than get bogged down on the details. Get the message.

Ever hear of the 2 minute rule? That rule states that you should not comment in a conversation that you just walked into unless you have listened for at least 2 minutes. Man, have I seen this violated. Time and time again I have witnessed people come in and dive right into a conversation without really understanding the context. It's kind of rude and foolish. You don't know where the conversation has been, or where it's going, so you should keep comments to yourself and listen to what's going on.

I was studying once and another person and I got into a debate about the meaning of a particular word. We were in a study area where people could come and go. As the conversation progressed several people came over and put in their two cents. This kind of irritated me because their two cents wasn't worth anything as far as I was concerned even if they were elder classmen. The other person I was studying with was reiterating the basic meaning of the word and I was saying that there was also a deeper meaning because the word related not only to the number of people it referred to but the difference as well. The person I was talking with kept repeating the same thing from a textbook and everyone was agreeing with her saying I was wrong and I should listed to the upper classmen. That rubbed me wrong as well. Anyway, I challenged them all on this and soon found the reference material to back me up and showed it to them. I also let them all have it for not listening to me and for butting in when they weren't welcome.

It seems easy for people to prescribe something when you say you have an ailment. Ever noticed how people who don't even know you will emphatically tell you what you need to remedy yourself and you are stupid for not following their advice. They may not have even heard all your symptoms and yet they draw a conclusion and prescribe treatment. Sometimes people just don't listen.

Have you ever had a conversation with someone that either has a distracting voice or their delivery is not that good? I've had teachers that were weak in their delivery, but the content was fantastic. Look for content, content, content.

Martin Luther King Jr's. famous "I have a dream" speech was one of the best deliveries I have ever heard. The speech was delivered in August of 1963 and was 17 minutes long. He calls for the end of discrimination and it is not until the very end of his speech does he use the now infamous phrase, "I have a dream." I would use that as an example of how a speech is to be delivered. It is incredibly well structured, the tempo is good and the emphasis is in the right places, and the cherry on the top is the phrase at the end that is a call to action.

When you are talking with someone you may notice how they struggle telling a joke, or demonstrate poor delivery. And yet others have trouble being engaging. Listen for the meaning and focus on the content of the message. Listening pays off. If you don't listen you will not gain vital information that can enhance your understanding of an area of life. Some people don't understand the value of listening and listening purposefully.

If I told you that I was going to give you the winning lottery numbers sometime in the next twenty minutes, you would hang on my every word. So what about when someone is talking to you? Do you just ignore them? Or do you pay attention?

Challenge:

Always listen for content. Don't get sidetracked by personality or redundancy or bad habits. Look for and listen for content.

You can improve your listening skills and it will pay off for you if you choose to do so. So distinguish yourself from the pack by listening to others when they speak.

7

Presenting your idea

At times you may be presenting an idea. It may be in a boardroom, office, home, park, car, bus, plane or any other place. The setting may be in front of hundreds of people or maybe just one. But if you have something you want to convey, you definitely want to do it in a way that it will be heard and we will talk a little about that in this chapter.

I remember the first time I spoke from a microphone publicly. Man, what a disaster. I prepared some witty things to say and some jokes but no one got my humor, the timing was bad, I kept repeating things, my mind went blank a couple of times. I could hear people snickering too. Ouch. After that I decided that I wasn't going to make that mistake again. One thing that caught me off guard was all the eyes staring at me. For me another thing that is challenging is just standing on stage and not being the one talking or doing something. Once I start having to do something, it's not so bad.

Presenting an idea can be done anywhere. If you want to do it effectively you must put some preparation into it. And the first thing I would say is that you KNOW YOUR SUBJECT MATTER. If you don't then why should anyone listen to you.

Preparation and research are a requirement if you are to be a subject matter expert, which should be your goal if you are going to talk about something. It's not a matter of guessing or going on feelings, but you must rely on facts. Politician's speeches are well written and rehearsed, albeit hot air, void of any real substance. You might as well believe the opposite of what they say half the time. I'm sure some of our politicians are well meaning, but it seems they all have an agenda that is not about me, but about them.

If you are presenting a product your company provides, you had better be a product expert. One of my first jobs in sales was selling computer networks. At the time I had almost no knowledge about how they worked or why my customers needed them. So my first few meetings were pretty basic. I studied hard to learn what I needed to and jumped into the job with both feet. Six months later it was a different story. Through persistence and hard work I was able to get a grasp on how I could market our services and found a niche market that I could sell to. I wouldn't call myself an expert, but I was pretty well informed and knew what I was talking about.

We set up a meeting with a group of technical users to market one of our newer computer software solutions. It was a little ahead of its time and would be considered clunk by today's standards. This particular product was new to me and the attendees of the meeting were unaware this technology was available. While the product was really cool and useful they were not ready to adapt to newer technology. As I showed the product, they all looked at me like I was from Mars and I found myself having a tough time speaking to why they would want it. Good thing we brought in lunch for them or they would have asked us to leave. In hindsight, I should have spent a lot more time in preparation and learning all the details and nuances of the system. Another thing I should have done was to talk to some people who were actually using it. Information from someone using the system would have been highly valuable.

CHALLENGE:

WHEN SELLING ANYTHING OR PRESENTING AN IDEA; TALK WITH SOMEONE WHO IS ACTUALLY USING IT AND GAIN FROM THEIR PERSPECTIVE HOW IT IS IMPACTING THEM. FIND OUT WHAT IT IS DOING FOR THEM AND HOW. USER TESTIMONIALS ARE MORE POWERFUL THAN YOUR WORDS.

If you are going to be meeting with a company, then you must do your homework. Know who the key players are, company history, challenges, competitors, what their strengths and weaknesses are.

A while back I had the privilege of speaking at an HR group function. It was a great bunch of people, mostly women, a few professors and other professionals. I tailored a presentation as if I was one of them. I was already aware of some of the challenges they faced and talked around those. Then I did a plug for my product. My presentation was peppered with questions that kept them engaged. By the end they all applauded and I spoke with several of them afterward. In subsequent meetings, they treated me as one of them. It was great to be recognized by this group and I enjoyed being a part of it. All I had to do was take a minute and relate to them. It paid off for me as I got some real insight into what was happening in the industry. Later, I was asked to speak at one of the universities. That was a good exercise for me because I had to prepare in light of where they were at in their studies. A couple of the students tried to grill me on my topic, but they weren't about to stump the master. I had a lot of confidence in that setting because I knew what I was talking about and was able to pass along some real life experience to those studying.

Something I have found useful is to know your limitations. Don't try and go beyond your area of expertise or open it up for questions if you are not prepared. You should be able to give your presentation in a fixed amount of time.

I used to practice this thing called an "elevator speech." It's sort of like that movie, "Working Girl", where the main character finds herself in an elevator with the president of the company and has to give her presentation on the spot and finish it before the elevator comes to a stop.

What I can tell you about working an elevator speech is that you have to be concise and get their attention fast. You only have a few seconds at the beginning where the other person is deciding if they are going to listen to you or not, so you'd better be ready. You should be able to give your elevator speech at a moment's notice. You never know when you will find yourself in a situation where you may need to give it and practice it as much as you can.

When putting your elevator speech together, you will want to develop a theme. Your theme will keep you on track. Your theme is something you will want to try and weave in and out of your conversation or speech. It also keeps you on point.

Be aware of yourself and your limitations and don't bite off more than you can chew. If you have never done a presentation in front of a large group, then get some help if you can. Prepare, rehearse, and then rehearse in front of people. My advice to you is to take it one step at a time. Don't over extend yourself. Stay within your scope of what you can handle. Avoid being arrogant and trying something just because you see someone else doing it.

Many times I have watched people do this effectively by utilizing this technique. When you make your points and substantiating points, always bring it back to the central theme. This isn't just for a board room meeting either, but can be used in any situation where you want to present your idea to someone else. Maybe you are convincing your child to attend college at a particular school because it will be the best for them, and then tell them why. Again it's about them! So your point or theme should revolve around them too.

Once I was doing a public presentation on "you get what you pay for." And I was talking about how businesses cut corners and get sidetracked on areas outside their core competency resulting in ineffectiveness. I had 5 major points I made in that speech and after each one, I said the phrase in a serious and low tone, "you get what you pay for." That was a great speech and I got lots of positive feedback on it. I kept going back to that theme and it also kept me moving in the right direction rather than veering off into another direction.

If you have something to say, then it is worth it to think it through and stick to your theme.

When you are preparing the presentation of your idea, here is a way to structure it so it will make sense. You want to break it down into four main areas.

Opening: This is where you set the stage for what is going to come. You may want to have an opening statement or hypothesis. Basically, this is where you tell them what you are going to tell them.

You want to make sure you don't begin with the conclusion. Instead, pose a question and lead the audience down a path to the answer. This will give you the opportunity to prove it in your presentation. Just like an opening statement, you want to give a summary and get them interested. Begin with an idea, a theme and build it for your audience. You also have to give them an idea of what's in it for them. Here is an example of an opening:

"Although people have been communicating for thousands of years, the need for effective communication in presentations has never been greater. Those who communicate effectively, are more respected and compensated accordingly. Have you ever felt like other people are not grasping what you are trying to convey? Ever struggled for the right words? I'm going to go through some pitfalls that many presenters fall into and show you a more concise way to present your ideas to others. Is there anyone who would not like to be better at presenting to an audience?"

Keep your opening to about two minutes. Whet their appetite and draw them into what you are about to share with them.

A few years ago the State of Florida felt that I needed to take a driving course to improve my knowledge of the laws and to make the roads safer for everyone that shared the road with me. Since I was invited, I accepted and attended. The class was about eight hours and was on a Saturday, UGH! But the kicker was how the presenter opened up the session by saying. *"Look, I know most of you don't want to be here and would like to be doing something else right now. And I have some bad news for you. The material I'm going to be sharing with you is solid and I believe in it, but the truth is, it's boring and there is no way I can make it interesting. So bear with me and try to stay awake."* Are you kidding me? It was bad enough already, but now I was doomed to eight hours of torture and there was absolutely NO WAY to make it interesting. That was like nails on a chalkboard for me. I do NOT believe that it had to be uninteresting and boring, which it was. But that's the fault of the presenter. With a mindset like that, it was all downhill from there.

Some things I try to avoid. Opening with a joke or humor. Unless you are a professional, keep your jokes to yourself. I've only seen a few speakers get away with using humor as a way to get things moving. I've done it a few times and you could hear crickets afterward. So use caution if you are planning to open this way.

You also want to focus on your audience by making eye contact with them. I'm not saying that you need to look everyone directly in the eye, but walk around the room as you speak. Also, go at the pace of the slowest person in the room. You can't afford to lose people. Make sure your audience is tracking with you. This can be done by asking questions about what you just said, giving away prizes for answering questions or having them raise their hands.

Body: This is the bulk of your presentation and where you build your case, proving what you said in your opening. You want to have a few points, and then back them up with facts or illustrations. Each subsection should have a single point and convey one idea relative to the theme.

One thing that may be helpful is to reinforce the theme by repeating a phrase that keeps you on point and is memorable when you have made a point. For example, based on my opening statement I used the word 'communication' several times. So when you make a point, you may want to pause and softly say the word "communication" or "communication is key." Or whatever suits your fancy, but you get the idea of driving your point home to your audience.

Summary: After your opening and the body of your message, you want to recap what you just told them as if it were in bullet points. Don't ramble here. Be concise and definitive about the points you made. It's your opportunity to restate your case and say, I told you I was going to show you such and such, and here is how I showed you, and this is why. Make sure it's brief and simple. And then prepare for your conclusion.

Conclusion: When it's all said and done, clearly state the conclusion and wrap it up. You may want to have a call to action or encourage a change in attitude or procedure. Whatever the case, keep this simple as well.

So many people have good ideas but don't put the effort into presenting them thoughtfully. It requires work, research and preparation. In the end, if you put the time in on the front end, you will be rewarded as a result.

CHALLENGE:

THE NEXT TIME YOU HAVE A PRESENTATION, HAVE TO TALK TO YOUR BOSS, OR EVEN YOUR CHILDREN, USE THIS MODEL AND PREPARE FOR IT.

Remember, these principles work whether you are presenting for a group of thousands, or having coffee with a friend. The more natural and conversational you can make it, the better the response will be.

8

Questions

Everyone wants to have the answers. Most feel important and smart when they have the answer. Look at children in school, how proud and excited they are when they have the answer. But what about the questions that lead to the answer. Questions are a huge key in conversation and connecting with another individual. Questions can help you get the focus off of yourself and on them, which is where it needs to be.

I was on a sales call with a new and energetic salesperson who was firing questions at a client. They were the type of questions that were meant to generate a response and generate interest in a solution we were selling. But it was more like an interrogation than a business meeting. The questions were rote, direct, impersonal, and predictable. I am surprised we weren't thrown out sooner than we were.

Once, while I was working in corporate America, an incident took place in which the details were ambiguous. HR got involved and they began a series of intimidating interviews with all employees. Because the details were extremely vague, it was more like a witch hunt rather than something that was supposed to be for the good of the company. The way it was presented put everyone on guard from the beginning and left everyone feeling defensive. In the end there was no real conclusion because the intention was unclear. You couldn't be sure where things were going, nor why this was taking place.

When they interviewed me I gave very guarded, non-committed responses. Halfway through the person conducting the interview told me that I sounded like Ollie North at a senate hearing. I told him that he wasn't going to get much more because the premise of this was unclear. No one knew who was involved in the situation, what was supposed to have happened, when the unknown incident took place and who reported it. So the results they got were scant and vague at best. In the end they told us that it was a waste of time and apologized for putting us through that.

You want better answers, <u>ASK BETTER QUESTIONS</u>.

Challenge:

If you are in sales, then develop 5 to 10 key questions that will help identify when someone would need your product or service and why.

If you want to ask better questions, it will require you to put careful thought into them. If you want to differentiate yourself, then you will have to go beyond the obvious and ask questions that produce the type of answer you are looking for.

If you were looking at new cars and had a few you were interested in purchasing, how would you respond to a salesperson coming up to you and asking, *"nice choice, I can see you in this car, what kind of payment did you have in mind."* The first words out of my mouth would be, NEXT! *You are the one who sells these things, you tell me how much the payments will be.*

Now wouldn't it be a lot better if the salesperson came up to you and said, *"that's a really nice car, tell me, what will you be using it for, to and from work, travel, and how many in your family?"* Now isn't that a WAY better question?

The way we ask questions will determine how the other person responds to us. It's always best to ask questions that will help you understand what the other person is really thinking and put them at ease. A major purchase like a vehicle is stressful enough without cheesy sales tactics. So put a little thought into a question before opening your mouth.

In a sales meeting you want to prepare questions that get to the heart of the issue. For example, if you are selling real estate, you would want to find out the main criteria for the buyer. Is it location, price, schools, size, new home or old, close to shopping or off the beaten path, how far they travel to work every day, what their plans are for the home in 5 or 10 years, will they need to sell it fast in a few years, or how many pets and what kind are they? As opposed to, what's you budget and when will you need to move?

So you see, asking better question requires a little deeper thought than the obvious and superficial ones that make you look like a cheap suit. It demands that we think them through cafefully and consider the outcome of a situation. There is more than one way of looking at things too. Look for new ways to view a situation rather than the same old way you always have. In doing so you will awaken new avenues and pathways to ask better, more precise questions.

I remember I was involved in a sales process that had taken several months and we were toward the end of the cycle. I had gotten a lot of resistance from the end users because of their unwillingness to consider making a change. This would involve some upheaval and change in their world at the beginning, but in the end it was going to solve a lot of problems for them. At the end of a demonstration, and after a barrage of questions that I already answered during the demo, I asked the question, so what else would you need to see in order to move forward with this? Truthfully I braced for more resistance. Part of me expected that they would want to talk to some of my customers, get some references, and a price reduction. This had been their pattern all along. From my perspective, this was a slam dunk and would work well for them, but again, I expected a fight. So as I asked the question *"What else would prevent you from moving forward?"*, the CEO proclaimed from the back of the room, "NOTHING." I almost fell off of my chair. So we paused for a moment and then signed the paperwork immediately, the deal was done. There was a bit of trouble at the beginning, but after the kinks were worked out I got a message from the CEO saying how pleased they were with the new system and how it benefitted them.

When I asked that question, I really did want to know what other things were holding them back from moving ahead with me. But I asked so I could remove any remaining obstacles and move on. But somehow I asked the right questions all along and listened to them.

Your prospects are being called on constantly. They're being hunted like wolves. Salespeople are calling and trying to sell them stuff. If you behave like everybody else, guess what? You'll get the same thing they are getting – NOT MUCH. Whenever you can, distinguish yourself from your competitors. Show them you are a notch above. And don't just say it – talk is cheap. Do something that someone else is not doing or go above in terms of service and follow up.

CHALLENGE:

ASK TOUGH QUESTIONS. ALL TOO OFTEN SALES PEOPLE HAVE HAPPY EARS AND HEAR ONLY WHAT THEY WANT TO HEAR. THEY ARE AFRAID TO ASK HARD QUESTIONS ABOUT WHY THEY WOULDN'T BUY FROM YOU OR WHY THEY WOULD NOT MAKE A CHANGE. DON'T BE AFRAID TO ASK THESE QUESTIONS, THEY CAN SAVE YOU LOTS OF TIME AND MAY HELP CLOSE DEALS.

Another thing to keep in mind: you never want to bash the competition. If you set yourself apart from them, you won't have to. The thing you want to do is to elevate yourself and your product. The professional athletes who achieve the highest levels of success don't whine about the bad calls, the poor performance of the rest of the team, coaching, fans, or whatever else. They focus on being better themselves.

In the 90's, the Detroit Red Wings Hockey team wase on the verge of greatness, but had a lot of disappointment because they had not lived up to the expectations set for them. After a tough loss, silence loomed in the locker room. The one to speak up was the captain of the team, who said, "I need to get better, yes we all do, but it starts with me." WOW, that's leadership. What if you took that approach with your job? What if you decided to be the very best you could be?

This goes back to doing things that others aren't in light of questions. It takes work, but by asking questions that others aren't, you are opening the door to answers that others aren't getting.

New answers demand new questions. Many breakthroughs have happened because people ask a new question. And in doing so, they got a different answer, maybe not the one they were expecting, but they got one.

As I was closing a deal with a client, I paused and asked what this would mean for them after it was fully implemented. He put his hand over a stack of folders and told me that these are projects he has put off for years and was hoping to complete before he retired in a few years. He told me that after his analysis that he would be able to free up an experienced, full time person for an additional 2 day a week and he would now be able to get to his projects. The expertise I was bringing to the table helped them not only be more efficient, but allowed them to focus on the task at hand.

A week later the highest ranking executive balked, which I anticipated, so I called for a meeting. During that meeting I looked him square in the eye and asked, "*How comfortable are you that an experienced employee is spending 60% of their time outside their area of expertise.*" He looked stunned and said, "*I never thought of if that way.*" Needless to say he agreed with me and moved ahead. In the end we spared them from a lot of headaches and relieved them of the burdens of regulatory compliance and filings. It was a great win for them.

There are occasions where it becomes necessary to ask questions that shock people in order to get their attention. You don't do this to be mean, but you do it to disturb them to a degree. To get them out of their comfort zone.

Let's talk a bit about the kinds of questions we ask, in particular open and closed ended questions. A great way to pair these types of questions is to ask open ended and then close with a closed ended one. Open ended can be used for gathering information, and close ended for gaining agreement or validation. You will want to use both, as neither is right for every situation and both have their place. Using these questions will yield a great amount of valuable data for you to be able to utilize.

On an appointment with a new client, I was a little nervous because I lacked critical information, which I should have had. But I thought I understood enough about them because I had similar clients and assumed they had the same needs and wants, so I forged ahead. The questions I asked were a lot of open ended and I tried to assume the sale. Big mistake. By lumping him in with others like him, I missed a lot that I could have gained from asking some open ended questions. Truth be told, I really didn't know much about his business nor where he wanted to go with it. But the biggest thing I missed was his reason to buy my product. I had all the reasons in the world that he should buy into my recommendation, but I neglected to recognize the reasons he would buy my product. The other thing is understanding what my solution would do for him. Those are the things that make our lives easier and set us apart from others. Just because you think someone should buy what you are selling, doesn't mean that they understand why they need it. A salesman's job begins with the word NO. If everyone said yes all the time you would simply be an order taker.

If your questions line up properly, they should lead you in the direction you want to go. If your destination is a sale, then what vital information do you need to obtain? You cannot rely on benefit based selling. To really connect with someone and provide the most value we must have a grasp of who will benefit, and what the product or service will do for them.

Don't assume you know what the answer will be either; you may be surprised what you find out. I see young salespeople fall into this trap all the time. They have a few questions that they think will lead to an obvious response. But it never goes quite the way they think it will, and they fall flat on their faces.

Challenge:

The next time you THINK you know the answer to why someone will agree with you, stop and ask a question to validate and get their perspective.

I was in a store some time ago and someone came up to me and started talking with me and I could tell he wanted to ask me something. He was asking about what I did so I told him and then he asks, *"Do you keep your business options open?"* I'll guess that about 95% of the people answer with 'yes.' Well not me. It took me a few milliseconds to smell a setup and I avoided it. So I replied, *"No I really don't because I have so much going on right now that anything else would be unproductive."* I could tell he was caught off guard and didn't know what to say. I'm sure the next question would have been something like, *"would you be interested in a business that requires no work, a small investment, and unlimited earning potential and there is no catch?"* Yeah, I have a bridge I'd like to sell you too.

Another time a friend called me out of the blue and asked, *"Do you like to travel and meet new people?"* Again I smelled a setup. I said, *"Look I have so much going on in my life I can't spare the time to travel, so no."* I wasn't lying. She was at a loss for words and fumbled for a couple of minutes. I wasn't being mean, just don't try to set me up and sell me using ridiculous questions like that. The way I see it, I saved us both a lot of time.

The next thing I'd like to focus on is follow up and probing questions. These are needed because you may ask a good question, but you need to go a little further in order to uncover information you need to help someone, make a sale, or clarify something.

As a parent we have all had our children go through the "why" phase. So they ask a question and no matter what the answer, they respond with "why?" Daddy, why is there air? Well so we can breathe. Why? So we can live. Why? So I can take care of you. Why? Because without me you'd be broke and homeless. Why? Because I make money to support you. Why? Ok, you get the drift.

In a professional sales position, you need to be like that. I had a sales executive give me some advice once that I haven't forgotten. He told me that when I go on sales calls to "*Be a detective.*" Find out everything I can. Get to the core issues of that business. I did it and I still do today. I have found it a powerful tool to have in my arsenal. Information is the most valuable thing you can have. It is the means to making an impact on your sphere of influence. So don't stop asking questions when you get a good response. Keep going and dig deeper, ask a follow up question and probe a little. Peel the onion back a few layers and find out what's underneath.

Utilizing questions is an unbelievable way to gather information and to focus on those in contact with you. Become a master at asking questions and you'll become a master at uncovering answers. The key is not having good answers; the key is having good questions. Remember that questions are the answer.

9

Why relationships matter more than facts

Have you ever lost a sale because your competitor was more tied into the business and decision makers than you were. We all have. Even when you have a much stronger business case and better price, you still end up getting the short end of the stick.

In life and in business we must focus our efforts, not on making friends or making sales, but building quality relationships. And as the premise of this book alludes to, it is about them and focusing your attention on them. Studies have shown that people are generally happier with other people. Relationships affect how we think, what we buy, what we do, where we live, and almost every area of our lives are impacted by our relationships. People buy more frequently from a friend than a stranger, right? Customer satisfaction is directly related to relationships.

I know for a fact that if any of my friends were using a competitor's product I could walk right in and sell them mine.

In a meeting with one of the finest restaurateurs I've ever known, I thought that I had the deal sewn up. I thought I developed good rapport with the owner and was on my way to making a sale. On a spreadsheet I had a comparison on the pricing side by side, and a list of the wins, as well as solid references. He agreed in principle to the solution and gave me a verbal yes. Man those can be lethal. So after two weeks of him going silent on me I called his assistant and she told me that my competitor came back in and renegotiated. Oh and he was an old friend. I never had a chance because relationships matter. And I clearly pointed out that his friend was making an excess of six thousand dollars for doing basically nothing. Still, in the end, I lost out.

I've been on the other end too and my customers with whom I have great business relationships with tell me that a competitor has come in threatening to cut their price and undercut me. Great, go ahead; give it away for all I care. Cut your profit to the bone. By doing that you devalue your product and commoditize yourself. You are just another salesman at that point and not a friend or trusted advisor.

The stronger your business relationship the better your retention will be. I used to take one of my clients out to lunch once a month on my dime just to be a friend. There was no monetary value in it, but I made a friend, and he would make calls for me to other companies telling them how good I was and how my solution helped them. Plus I was able to gain his insight from a customer perspective as to how my approach and product benefited them. So, now I can talk to a prospect in terms of how they would be able to use it, rather than a data dump and hoping that something I said addresses what they need.

When you run into a situation where an incumbent has done a good job and taken care of the client, you either have to have something that the competitor doesn't, or you are going to have to wait your turn. They won't easily discard a solid business relationship, and why should they? When you find a good vendor, you'd better keep them happy too. It takes work to develop a good working business relationship. Don't think for a second that you are just going to waltz into someone else's account, throw around a few catch phrases and expect business to come your way. You've got to earn it. Keep this in mind. If you walk in the first time and you get a list of your competitor's prices, you may win that business, but don't you think that they will do that to you too?

Challenge:

Visit 3 customers you have already sold and get an idea from them exactly WHAT your product/service is doing for them and how it impacts them. Get a story.

At times, you may show up at the right time and provide something that they need right away or maybe they are unhappy for whatever reason, and then you can be a hero.

Relationships are forged over time and based on ethical practices. You don't have to build them that way, but when you don't, they won't last and in the end it will not be the kind of relationship you want anyway. You cannot built a solid relationship based on dishonesty, greed, compromise or anything of that sort because it will come back to haunt you.

When I was a freshman in high school there was a kid that was picking on me and I was getting tired of it. He was older and a lot bigger than me, but I was sick of his insults and negative attitude toward me. After a few days I was walking to school with a new friend who I felt I could trust, so I confided in him. I told him I was tired of this guy's bullying and I was done taking it. The second I arrived at school that guy walked up to me and said, "I hear you want to fight me?" I thought to myself, great, what a friend that guy turned out to be. We agreed to settle our differences across the street from school property so neither of us would get suspended. As the day ended I was heading toward the agreed place and I swear the entire school was there waiting to see the fight. For a second I wished that I had kept my mouth shut, but then I saw my adversary and he suspected I would dodge out on him and not show up. He obviously didn't know me very well. So we had it out and it came to a draw. At first I was mad that I didn't win, but a bunch of older kids came up to me and congratulated me for standing up to that bully who was twice my size. And from then on, the attitude was gone too. In that incident, I fixed one problem relationship and discontinued another.

Relationships require maintenance. Just because people say you are likable, doesn't mean that everyone will like you. You have to get the attention off of yourself and engage with them. In short, you must get the focus off yourself and on others.

They say that people buy from people like them. Partially true; actually they buy from people they like and from people they trust. Both elements take time to develop and nurture. So show yourself friendly, willing to go the extra mile and do what you say you are going to do. That will build trust with the client and you may make a friend. When a good salesperson shows up to visit a client, he's like a family member or old friend is coming through the door. They are really glad to see him instead of gritting their teeth and murmuring under their breath, *"not him again."*

How do you get people to like you? Well that's a tough one and I don't think there is a definitive answer. However in the words of Napoleon Hill, one of the things he lists as keys to prosperity, that it's important that to have, *"a pleasing personality."* What does that mean? Well, I believe that depends on the other person.

One of the things I teach in my sales training classes and seminars is to mirror your customer. This is not to be done out of any motive other than genuinely endeavoring to connect with your client. Any time you are talking with another individual you have the opportunity to learn something from them and you should try and mirror them to make an association. The natural chemistry when we do this will lend to more open and honest communication. This is not some Jedi mind trick, but a way of focusing on the other person in a conversation. You can mirror the tone, gestures, eye contact but it is not to be done in a mimicking way that would insult them. Just be aware of who they are and what they are like and immerse yourself in the conversation.

Not saying that by doing this that everyone will instantly like you, but it's a way you can be like them.

Challenge:

In a conversation, stop and notice the body language of the person you are talking with. Is it open or is it closed? This will reveal a lot about how they feel relative to what you are saying.

What about trust? Well, that doesn't come instantly. It comes with time, effort, and proving yourself being trustworthy. It may be sped up by our reputation, but that is earned over time as well.

Over the years people have reached out to me as a result of an acquaintance that has done some business with me. I took care of them and they feel comfortable in recommending me. Many great business relationships have some out of referrals. They refer you because they trust you. So don't take that for granted and that should be your goal in relationships.

Ever hear the phrase **your reputation precedes you**? Well it does. Once I was sitting with a couple of business owners to discuss some consulting work. A couple of their business advisors told them to call me and that I could help them. We laughed for a bit and I wasn't surprised when the deal was finalized. This was one of those situations where I was well suited for the task and there was no way I could screw it up. Afterward they told me what the people referring me said to them. They were no slouches themselves and I was flattered at the things they said about me. My habit was to extend myself to those advisors and made an impact in their business. So when the time came, they were more than happy to return the favor. Not only that, there was an element of them pre-selling the value I would bring to their organization. It was like they were insisting they at least talk to me.

When I build my business relationships, or any relationship for that matter, I NEVER try and look at it from the perspective of what I can gain, but I look at building a friendship based on honesty and trust. These are the building blocks upon which great things are forged.

I've set up several business networking groups designed to benefit everyone involved. One group included a compliance advisor, a banker, a CPA, a financial advisor, a benefits broker, and comp broker. These are the main people a CFO would meet with and the idea was that if we were all calling on the same people anyway, why not work together and help each other since there was no overlap in our offerings. Working together made things easier and we helped each other succeed Now, I was particular about the people I allowed into these groups, and they had to be the kind of people I wouldn't hesitate referring to my family. This made the selection process simple. As a result I made several large sales that I wouldn't have otherwise been able to. When we would meet, each of us would share what was happening in our industry. Then we would each bring a list of 5 businesses that we think would be a good fit for our services, but had not been able to get any traction. It was a great way to get warm introductions and help our clients by introducing them to business partners that can help their businesses.

No matter what the facts are, relationships will get you further than facts alone. The facts themselves without the relationship can be sterile and people can have trouble believing in them. Without a relatable story or compelling reason to listen to you, they may or may not hear you.

10

Dreams

Everyone has dreams. Each person has a unique vision for what they dream of. How can you realize your dreams? What have you dreamed for yourself? What dreams do you have for others in your life? Dreams can become reality if we persist, have a little creative thinking and a strong belief.

So I have to ask, what is your vision for your life? Where do you see yourself? The picture you hold of yourself with clarity is who you are. If you see yourself in a positive light, then you will draw those positive things to you, the same is true for negative thinking and attitude.

Where do you see yourself in 5 years? The more specific we can be about our dreams, the clearer the results will be. What kind of lifestyle do you want for others around you? What do you want to be able to give or contribute to those around you?

How do you see people around you? Do you see their true potential or do you see their limitations. Do you see possibilities or obstacles? I believe that we should look for the best in people and see them in a positive light. That doesn't mean that we ignore negative or destructive behavior, but in general you should see other people succeeding. If you enjoy seeing someone else fail or something bad happen to someone else, you are feeding off of negatives and will bring the same upon yourself.

I've worked around people who think this way. They laugh when others stumble at the trials of life. That's no way to live. Take the high road and don't fall into the endless void of gossip and backbiting. If you want good in your life, give good to others and just plain give – freely.

When I was moving my family to a new city, I had the opportunity to choose where I wanted to work. So where do I start? Good question. I decided that I wanted to be in sales so I grabbed a phone directory and called the place where I wanted to work. After I spoke to the operator, a recruiter came on the line and I said "Are you looking for a talented salesperson?" His reply was, "Always." I said, "Great, when can I come in and talk to you." We made arrangements to come in and interview, take personality tests, mock sales calls, more interviews, additional tests, more interviews. After about a month, the highest ranking executive asked me to come down for one last interview. In my mind I thought I already had the job. I sort of respectfully told him to quit messing around and hire me. Further I said that I will make my mark on the company and he should not risk losing me to a competitor. He conceded and said I was the only one he ever hired without a face to face meeting.

I had a vision for what I would accomplish there, and exceeded my expectations during my employment. I exceeded theirs too. That executive and I joked about that phone call at several award banquets and he readily admitted that he was glad he made the exception. I flourished in that environment and am grateful for my time there. At the time I worked there, it was an excellent place to work and I made some of the best friendships in my life; many of whom I still am in contact with until this day.

You see, I had a vision for the type of work I wanted to do and what I would accomplish. I saw that job as a way for me to get there. They gave me a lot of support and great mentors to follow. The position allowed me to maximize my talents and grow professionally. One last thing, my supervisors all saw the potential in me and set me up for success. Their vision for me was a top producer. One of my managers referred to me as one of the 'elite' sales reps on the floor. That made me feel pretty good because I respected him and I knew he meant it.

I have a vision for my children, and if you have children I'm sure you do too. I see them accomplishing far more than I ever did and being the very best people they can be. I believe that they will be able to maximize their talents and abilities. If there is anything I can do to nurture their abilities, I will make sure it happens.

We can have vision for what we can do for people too. Working with some top law firms, I would lay out a vision for what my solutions would do for them and how it would make them more efficient. As I would tour the office, I could see them using my system to help save time and money.

CHALLENGE:

WHEN WAS THE LAST TIME YOU DARED TO DREAM? WHEN WAS THE LAST TIME YOU HAD A REALLY GREAT VISION OF YOURSELF AND YOUR SITUATION? YOU CAN CHANGE THAT MINDSET BY DEVELOPING A POSITIVE VISION FOR YOUR LIFE. ENVISION YOUR LIFE THE WAY YOU WANT IT TO BE.

One particular deal involving technology services to a company, I became aware that there was a person that literally could not go on vacation because of how she had to be around to run payroll and manage the banking accounts. I told her that this system would allow her to go on vacation because of the automation. After it was up and running I checked back with her and she told me that she finally took a vacation. That made me feel really good. She had no vision for that before I came along and opened their eyes and showed them how things can be.

Having a vision for yourself, for others, for how things can be, will go a long way to your success. So practice it as much as you can and help them dream.

Of all the long suits in your life, what are your top talents? What are the things you excel at? As you live your life, you should become aware of what they are. Focus on what you are good at and endeavor to do something in life that makes the most of your strengths. There are many books and publications that can help you decipher what you are best suited to do. So figure out what they are and put them to work. Be clear on exactly what they are and how you can use them in life and business.

I have taken many personality profile tests and I usually get results that peg me for being successful in sales. That doesn't mean I will automatically be an instant success. I have to work at it every day. But some of those tests will reveal specific aptitudes and abilities that I can focus my efforts on to be my best.

When I was looking for part time work, I applied for a job that sounded interesting. The ad read, *"get paid to jog, good money, flexible hours, $10 per hour."* I called the number and they gave me a time to go in there and interview. It was a job where I'd be running, so I actually put on my running attire and ran there. When I showed up in their lobby, there was at least 30 people sitting around in suits and for a moment I felt out of place. I walked up to the receptionist and gave her my name and she asked me to fill out an application, so I sat back down and filled out. When I was done, I gave it back to the receptionist and cracked a joke and she told me that they would be in touch with me and I left. I thought I had no chance for getting this job, which was basically running in selected neighborhoods putting flyers in mailboxes. It sounded like a dream job. Two days later they called me back for another interview and this time they TOLD ME to wear my running attire. So again I did. It turns out that the first interview was the interview. They were looking for someone who looked the part of a jogger, and someone who was pleasant. The girl who was sitting at the desk was making notes and observing how pleasant the applicants were. They were concerned about first impressions. Obviously I got the job and really liked it. But what was even better was the fact that I did something that I was good at and that fit my schedule.

Make a list of your top talents; maybe ask someone else what they feel your talents are. This will help you narrow what you do and how you can add value to your sphere of influence.

When you figure out what you want to do or want in your life, and develop a roadmap. How are you going to get there? What is it going to take? How long will it take? Who will need to be involved? What will have to happen to make this a reality? What resources will be needed?

When you are driving to a particular destination, don't you want the directions to be clear? Of course you do. So why not draw out a clear roadmap to something that is important to you? It's not as complex as you think. I was traveling across country with a friend a few years back. Along the way, we would be traveling near my brother's house and then my mom's, so we planned the entire trip and padded a few days in there to spend time with my family. We planned out all of our stops, what we would bring, what we would need, and how much gas and money we would need to make it there. It was a wonderful trip and the time with my family was great. If we had not planned everything so carefully, then we would have not enjoyed it as much and wouldn't have got as much out of it.

Drawing out a good roadmap will help you get the most out of your time and resources. Those who fail to do so will miss out and not get to where they want to go, or at least take longer to get there and expend more resources.

Challenge:

When setting goals, incorporate the appropriate steps and anticipate what will be needed. In other words, don't just say you want more business, get concrete and be clear as to how much business and *how* you are going to get it.

The first thing to be clear on when developing your roadmap is your **destination**. Where do you want to wind up? Many people fail to become clear on this and will have unclear results. So, just to say I want to be wealthy is not specific enough. You have to answer a lot of questions prior to achieving "wealth." Any financial advisor would tell you that in order to obtain (and retain) wealth it requires a solid plan. He would ask you; How are you going to get the money? How much would you save? How much do you invest? What purchases would you have to make? What will you do to protect your earnings? What specific amount do you want to make? How long will this take? What percentage will you devote toward the goal? What is your backup plan? What about college? And that's just the beginning. Then you would set up a plan to make that happen based on historical data as well as realistic earning and market potential. Form there you implement the plan, and you are supposed to stick to it, but what if your needs change? Or what if something unexpected happens? Then you will have to evaluate your priorities and see if you want to stick to your plan or make adjustments. Then continue toward your goal, and stick to it. Realize that it's a marathon, not a sprint.

So, that is one example of developing a roadmap. Start from the destination and work backward to where you are now and plan all the steps in-between. Try and think of everything you will need and plan for things that may come up, including obstacles.

Every January I notice a lot of new people at the gym. They are not too hard to spot. I believe that these people have good intentions, and mostly trying to make good on New Year's resolutions. Some jump on the cardio machines, some try weights, and some get the expert advice of a trainer. By the end of the month, very few, if any, are sticking to their plan. Getting your body in shape after years of inactivity is difficult, but not impossible. Studies have shown that if you can stick to a regular routine for six months, you will more than likely stick with it the rest of your life. But the problem is that people bite off more than they can chew (no pun intended). They want the pounds to come off after a week or so and they get frustrated. If you want to lose 30 lbs., then plan on losing 5 pounds a month for 6 months. That's a realistic goal. And also, make a schedule of going to the gym at specific times during the week and treat that time like it's the most important thing you are doing. Also, you should incorporate a healthy diet and integrate that piece into your goal.

Something to keep in mind when setting goals is that, if others can be successful then so can you. You have a ton of potential and can achieve great things. If you want to reach new heights, then find someone who has had success in an area that you would like to, find out what they did to achieve success, and do the same thing.

There are million dollar producers in the insurance business. They are an elite bunch and highly recognized in the industry. If I was in the insurance business and wanted to reach that plateau I would get with one of those producers, find out as much as I could about what they did to get to where they are and get busy doing the same.

All of my career, I've observed successful people and tried to imitate what they did right. I would talk to them and ask them about how they approach their day, how they prospect, prepare for appointments, and what they don't do. You wouldn't believe how much that information can help you. Don't reinvent the wheel, glean from what you can from those top performers and begin thinking how they do immediately.

One thing I have found that helps promote an environment for success is having the right motivation. The will to be rich for the sake of being rich will only bring sorrows. Have you heard the stories about people winning the lottery only to lose it all and forced to declare bankruptcy? It is tragic but avoidable. The chief culprit is motive of heart. People want to win all that money but don't have any idea what to do with it, other than to spend it all and enjoy the supposed finer things in life. They really don't have a noble purpose and vision for what they could do.

Another way of looking at this is to define your purpose. What do you want to obtain with the sum of money? Will you purchase property? Toys? Save? Buy a company? To define your purpose will give you clarity and strength to continue when things get tough. So dream big, and keep your motivation and purpose in mind.

Take the opportunity to brainstorm with others when you can. Bounce your ideas and dreams off of others. Freely accept input (not negativity) and be willing to reshape your dream to make it realistic for you to achieve it.

This is where you have an opportunity to factor in others when it comes to your dreams.

Do the proper research. When I was setting up my construction company, I talked with people in the industry, suppliers, contractors, competitors, laborers, and gathered as much information as I could. Like I said earlier, DON'T REINVENT THE WHEEL.

When you decide on your goal, act as if you can't fail. Proceed as if you have already achieved your goal. Believe in yourself and that you will absolutely reach your destination. In the words of the great Napoleon Hill, author of Think and grow Rich, *"Whatever the mind can conceive and believe, it can achieve."*

There may be people around you that are negative about your dreams, get rid of them. Like dust off your feet. You don't have to be mean, but if someone isn't helping you, they are hindering you. Don't let their poisonous words pierce your soul. Spend time with people who are supportive of you and want to see you succeed.

Lastly on this topic of dreams, see it every day. When I was a child, my family would plan a trip to an amusement park in the summer. To build it for us, my parents would tell us about the rides we would be able to experience. Even though it was months away we would anticipate it every day and look forward to it and imagine how much fun we would have. And when we finally got there I was so excited and wanted to do everything I imagined.

Our dreams are like that too. We should never stop dreaming of new things to do and accomplish in our lives. Every day can be an exciting adventure. Remember, yesterday is history, tomorrow is a mystery and today is the present, and that's why it's a gift.

11

Connect the Dots

    Surely you've heard the phrase, outside the nine dots. The first time someone asked me to connect the nine dots; I first thought it would be a piece of cake. Then he said, "Do it by drawing no more than four straight lines and without lifting your pencil." HHHmmmmm. Why did you have to make it so hard, that changes everything. As if it were an act of futility I attempted a few times and finally gave up. Afterward the secret was revealed and THEN it seemed so obvious. It was one of those times you feel silly because in reality it was very simple.

    Now I don't want to give the secret away if you haven't tried it, but most people don't leave the imaginary square when drawing the lines. The point is that in order to get things done, you have to look at things differently and see beyond the imaginary borders.

Some of the greatest innovations in our world today have come by people thinking outside the norm, looking at possibility and not limitations. Innovation requires asking different and better questions of ourselves and others.

When I worked for a company that was a leader in a particular industry, they were known for their cutting edge technology but the weakness was customer service. So what do you think I focused on? Yes, technology and the improvements automation would bring to them. Then a few years later I worked for a smaller competitor in the same industry. This company had mediocre technology that didn't show very well, but could get the job done in most cases, but the strength was customer service. So I positioned that company as a business partner with outstanding customer service. That was my focus.

So was that dishonest? NO. I focused on the strengths of both companies and not the weaknesses when I marketed to companies which would be a good fit.

My aim was to connect with companies that needed the service and then illustrate how it would help them. I connected the dots with the offering I had at the time and focused my energies on promoting the strengths. I didn't ignore the weaknesses, more like made sure I could deliver and put together a package that would help them function better based on what they required.

<u>One of the worst mistakes I've ever seen in years of presentations</u>: I was working on a very large and complex deal. The homework had been done, with very little help from my team and there I was ready to present my system and solution. I brought in food and warmed up with a recap. Then the "so-called" expert doing the presentation began at the first screen and said, "Now, this particular functionality

isn't presently available, but we will have it someday." This capability was important to the customer and to start out by saying that, oh yeah we can't do what you want was unbelievably wrong. It was like the air was let out of the room. When I heard this I was mortified and I was a little hacked off. If I were Spiderman I would have webbed her mouth shut. I NEVER used that useless person for my sales calls again. If you are going to make it about them, then try and find something they need and show them how you will connect the dots between what you have and what they need. Also, I learned not to bring inferior people on my sales calls so they could sabotage them. I think she took the leftover food with her too. That was like adding insult to injury. Needless to say, we didn't stand a chance of getting the business and many hours of my time went down the toilet.

When I followed up with the CEO, he told me that he felt I was professional and that I understood my product and their company, but because of the weak and unprofessional demo of the software he could not overcome the objections of everyone in the room.

Some things I learned were this: Focus on your strengths; understand what you have and how you can help them. Be solution oriented. Concentrate on the impact of your solution – what will you ultimately do for them. And expose the deficiencies in how they are doing business presently. Show a before and after to draw a contrast they can relate to.

Challenge:

When you are making a point with someone, try and help them connect the dots for themselves rather than tell them why they should think like you do. Remember, telling is not selling.

Another time I was meeting with a successful owner of a restaurant chain. He was using an antiquated system and they were bogged down with inefficiencies. The gentleman was kind and was very open with me about what he wanted. He wanted some specific things: Compliance; Automation, Integration. All of these were in my wheelhouse, although I had to piece together a solution that was end to end. Several people and third party vendors were involved and I had to get them to work together. In my final presentation, I took a large board and drew a cartoonish picture of how the data would flow. I checked and rechecked that this would work and tested it. It was solid. When I went back for the final meeting I was prepared and confident. A big difference was that I was in control of all of the moving parts and rechecked every detail prior to the final presentation. This was a win/win. I saved them 2 ½ man days every week and gave them better data. You might say that in my meetings with him, I connected the dots and showed him a clear picture of how it would change his business, but it didn't ring true until I drew that cartoon picture for him so he could see it. It worked. The deal was large and implemented seamlessly.

Connecting the dots is more complex than just dumping data and hoping something sticks. You've got to first connect with them and see their world from their perspective. Take off your shoes so you can put on theirs, then walk around a little bit to see what life is like from their viewpoint. Few business professionals really do this.

Once you understand what they need, you cannot have a chance to put together something that works for them. Customize your solution with them in mind and present it in a way they will appreciate it. You have to make sure it fits, like a hand in a glove. A true salesperson is a trusted business consultant who understands his product thoroughly and knows what it will do for customers – he also knows how to put the two together for a client. If you don't really have something that would be the best for them, then it's time to move on and find someone else who needs what you have to offer.

In order to connect the dots we don't just walk around spewing out buzz words that we don't understand. You have to make a connection with the other person - yes a person. If you are selling to companies, you are not meeting with a faceless, corporate entity. Behind every company is a person and behind every sale there is a person. You have to figure out what they want and see if it matches with what you have.

Ever see someone in a suit or dress that is a little too tight? No one told them that it doesn't fit. Maybe you should know when your product or service doesn't fit either.

But if it does, then connect the dots for yourself and then show them. One time I was consulting for a large corporation and was scheduled to meet with one of their teams at another location. So we walked over to the remote location where there were hundreds of people in cubicles and there was a buzz in the air. I was a few minutes early. The meeting was to begin at 5pm and it was about 4:50 when I reached the conference room. There were about 10 people in the room, so I walked right in, slapped my notepad on the table and jokingly said, "You are all probably wondering why I called this meeting." I've done this dozens of times and it always breaks the ice. But this time was different; there was stone cold silence. Everyone sat there in silence for a second, I didn't even notice. So I introduced myself. Then they all did. Well, the meeting had begun. Or had it? Then one person very kindly asked, "*Why are you here?*" After a nanosecond I got that uncomfortable feeling like I was in the wrong place, then it hit me, this meeting was probably going on since 4pm and was not the 5pm meeting I was expecting. I said, "*WOW, how embarrassing, I'm sorry for having interrupted.*" Then everyone cracked up at the obvious misunderstanding. Word of that got around fast and it was a good laugh. So, I connected the dots fast once I heard the words, "why are you here." Then I exited as soon as I could. In about one minute I made a memorable entrance as well as a fantastic exit.

Later that week, I was tested on my knowledge of how to connect the dots for a customer, and I flew through it because I listened and remembered. My ability to add value was tied to how I understood WHAT the product would do for businesses. Then you can relate to another in a business situation.

Remember those commercials for Ginsu knives. They'd show numerous uses, how much time it will save you and how it will improve the quality of your life. Those spots were fast, flashy and gave you a ton of information in a few seconds. They assume you need it – NOW! But commercials are sort of fishing for customers by machine gunning the public and making people think their product will change their lives. They have to anticipate or assume what potential customers will want in advance and tie it to their product. The world of advertising is like that. However, in the real world of sales, we have to hear it directly from them in order to build our business case.

CHALLENGE:

CATCH YOURSELF WHEN YOU ARE IN MACHINE GUN MODE. DON'T SIMPLY FIRE AWAY AND ASSUME THAT OTHERS WILL SEE THINGS THE WAY YOU DO. ASK QUESTIONS TO VALIDATE THAT THEY ARE WILL YOU AND ARE TRACKING WITH YOU.

When meeting with someone initially and you are discovering what they need, it's wise to NOT jump the gun the second you hear something you can do. Be patient and ask about why something is important to them. For example; I was on a sales call once where the customer was pointing out what they needed and my manager, who had less experience than me, chimed in and said, "yes, we can do that." It was sort of like raising her hand to say, "Me too, me too." STOP! Do NOT just give a pat answer, and say, "yes, yes, we have that too." Then you are just like everybody else.

When someone asks a car salesman a question like, "Does this car have windshield wipers?" Your response could be, "Are windshield wipers important to you?" They may either answer with a 'yes', or they may give additional detail. So, dig a little further, "Does your current vehicle have windshield wipers?" If yes, "OK, what would you change about what you have?" They will most likely give additional information; so you could follow up with, "So how would these impact your life?" I know this is an oversimplification, but you should get my drift. Dig and follow up. You see, this will help you later when you are able to tell them what they said to you about how these would benefit them.

Another day I was on a sales call with a well prepared system engineer and as he was showing functionality of the system, heads were nodding, and I was taking notes. During my final presentation I mentioned all of the items in which they nodded their heads. That hit the nail on the head because I knew those things were important to the end user. When I went to ask for the business, I was not surprised when I got absolutely no resistance. I told the person doing the presentation for me that I was glad he was there and thanked him for being so well prepared. He really identified with the pain felt of the people having to do all the manual work and showed them how it would give them what they want and be easy to use.

Connecting the dots for people isn't hard if you listen to them and get where they are coming from. It's just a few steps, and you'll be glad you took the time to do it for them.

12

Your words

It's been said that words are more powerful than the edge of a sword. They can sway people or tear them down to the ground. Words can set people free or encase them. What kind of words will you choose? You have the power to decide. Will they be compelling or will they fall to the ground. They will also be revealing about yourself to others.

Everyone likes friends and most people want others to like them. Choose your words wisely and you will have plenty of friends. I am speaking of words, but more exactly, the meaning behind them. Positive words will go a long way with people and contribute to their overall well-being. So ask yourself, how are my words affecting other people? What kind of message do they send?

I worked with a salesperson that, upon first impression, I thought was talented. He was dynamic, confident, energetic, well spoken, and had a reputation for being a hell of a salesman. He also had a reputation for pushing the envelope a little, which didn't bother me, but I was aware of it. One day I was on a sales call with this individual. What I saw was a total lack of integrity; he was pushy, dishonest, and disrespectful to the customer. Nothing he did was criminal, but I'm confident that no company would want their reputation to suffer with someone like that on the payroll. When I got back to the office the sales manager asked me what I thought of him. I said, "*Do you really want to know?*" He said he did, so I told him what I thought and that I never wanted to be associated with him in any way again. The next day he was fired for unethical sales practices. His words and his message were cheap, unprofessional, his practices were deceitful and he treated the customer as if they were stupid. People like him are a dime a dozen and have absolutely no place in a professional sales environment.

I take pride in myself and want to have a good reputation with my co-workers, superiors and my clients. And for the most part I believe that I do. I word hard on my reputation and try and say what I mean and mean what I say. One thing I have never done is simply try and tell people what they want to hear. That's not how to build a great reputation as a business professional. They have to know they can trust you, rely on you, that you will back up what you say and do what you say.

I heard someone say one time, "Your actions are speaking so loud I can't hear what you are saying." Words are great, but without supporting action, they are meaningless. One thing I have found rampant in the business community is lack of follow through. I've been guilty of it too, but I have also learned from my mistakes.

      I used to have a policy where if a customer called me back to make an unfavorable change or complain, I wouldn't immediately return the phone call. Rather I would wait for them to call me back a second time. I guess I thought that sometimes people would react emotionally and call to complain without thinking it all the way through, or that if it was REALLY important they would call me back again. WOW, was I wrong. What I found is that by the time they called me back they were really angry and felt neglected. I have since changed my practices because it is a horrible way to treat anyone, especially customers who are paying you.

      I had a goal of contacting everybody in my database every quarter. Now I had it in my mind that some of the prospects just weren't going to ever buy from me, but I gritted my teeth and made myself do it. Low and behold, one of the five companies I had on a special list that I thought would never buy, asked me to come in for a meeting. When I met with them they said that they really appreciated my persistence and that one of the things they look for is good follow up. As we went through a process I uncovered that there were many areas that I could affect and improve. In two weeks I closed the deal and they were a good client for many years. They even served as a referral for me on numerous occasions.

Challenge:

Have you pre-judged people or your own customers? Do you think you know how they will respond in advance? Challenge yourself to NOT do that and act as if they will respond favorably.

Had I not been true to my words I would not have earned that business. Also, if I had not followed up, I would not have earned their respect and the right to win the account. I spoke earlier that you cannot prejudge people or businesses, so don't. So many times I have been surprised when someone seems to change their mind and buy from me. And other times I have known for sure that I was going to make a sale only to come up short. It's frustrating sometimes, but that's sales.

I was calling on a rather large regional company that was very well known and somehow I got in touch with the right person and got a meeting. At first I was a bit nervous because this company was about 10 times larger than the average size we normally dealt with. But I went ahead and met with them, getting familiar with the landscape of the company. Initially there were some glaring deficiencies that I was pretty sure I could fix. Before opening my mouth I kept silent and gathered more information. The last thing I wanted to do was to ruin my reputation by saying we can do something that we would not be able to live up to. I even scheduled a trip for them where we could investigate the complexities of their requirements further. These all went really well. I was told that I was the frontrunner and I was pretty excited. There was one little thing relating to integration which required a "work around." When I shared the specifics with them, I walked them through the process in painstaking detail. To me it wasn't that big of a deal in light of the whole scheme, but to them it was just too big of a gap and they went another direction. In hindsight we were sort of out of our league. What kept us in play was the way I managed the process with integrity and competence. They liked me, the company, the concept, the service, but a piece of the technology was severely underdeveloped and lacked the depth it should have had. When I got the news that my company want not selected I was a bit disappointed, but when I looked back I felt like I could be proud of the job I did. It also led to a great referral.

My words meant something to them and my honesty was evident. To them, I was someone whom they would, and did, recommend to other people. I managed the process correctly. During the process a competitor didn't dig very deep into the needs of the reporting complexity and plowed through the details of what the requirements were. They actually began implementing with them, but the process was halted because they were not forthcoming about how the integration would work with the existing system. They will not have a chance to earn that business for a long, long time. The competitor was thrown out in disgrace and they will not be trusted again by those with whom he was trying to sell.

In smaller business communities you have to have a solid business reputation. Word gets around fast. Unfortunately bad news seems to travel faster than good news. So say what you mean and follow through. Make sure your words mean something.

I believe that we get what we give. If we give a lot of negativity we will receive a lot of it for ourselves. If we are dishonest and take short cuts, we will get back the same. You get what you give. No way around that. Make your words kind, positive and meaningful. What you do and what you say is a reflection on you. To be able to control and impact your reputation is squarely on your shoulders. Treat your words as if they are the gems that they ought to be and make them count. Remember that your words can either build or tear down. Consider how you want to be perceived and direct your words accordingly.

13

Not everyone is like you

So many times people disagree on issues. They go on and on about how they feel about an issue, whether it is religion, politics, business, social, or whatever category you like. Each has their point, which to them seems obvious and logical. They debate and banter. And it seems as if the more they argue, the greater the divide is. Both sides dig in and strengthen their position and neither budges. Nothing really gets resolved in these situations and neither side gains an appreciation for the other.

So why are there so many opinions out there? Why can't people see a logical point when it is so obvious? People become closed off sometimes when they feel strongly about an issue. When emotions become involved in an idea it is more difficult to consider thinking in a different way. Emotions color our thoughts in a way that nothing else can. It is vital that we keep that in mind when we are dealing with others. They feel strongly for a reason; so try and understand why they feel the way they do. It would be better if they each listened to the other and maybe tried to appreciate where the other is coming from.

One thing that drives me crazy is being late and waiting. When I was a child, my dad was always late. Late picking me up, late arriving and it left me waiting many, many times. I hated rushing and the stress of driving like a madman to get somewhere at a certain time and knowing that we would arrive late and unprepared. This happened habitually and the lack of preparation and not having a cushion drove me up a wall. To this day I am always on time and HATE being late. I see it as disrespectful when people do it to me.

My years as a sales professional have shown me a lot about how people are and how they treat others. About 99% of the time, when people have to reschedule or they stand me up, they apologize and will make it right by meeting with me.

One of my best friends and closest associates is a southern gentleman and is somehow challenged in being punctual. He will arrive, but he may be late, or on the phone when he walks into the meeting. When I first met him I didn't understand how he could be so inconsiderate of people's time. And at one point I thought that we wouldn't be able to be business partners because I equated his habits with being lackadaisical and unprofessional. However he did live in the south and things move at a different pace. I can be very intense and direct, and he is too, but in a very different way.

So after a few meeting and having to reschedule a few times, we lost touch. A while later I decided to see if we could work together again, so I struck up a meeting and we talked. This time I did not expect him to be like me, but endeavored to view things from his perspective. Then I finally got it. He was just a really busy man, with a lot of irons in the fire and trying to manage a ton of activity with limited support. He has a great personality and a good sense for business, but he was different in his approach toward others than I was. And guess what? THAT'S OK.

Once I was sitting in a meeting and it was about a half an hour in and here he comes, late as usual (he did have a long drive). He tried to make a subtle entrance, without avail, then his phone rings and we all laughed. They too had seen what I had, he is a great person, a hard worker that knows how to produce.

Since I took the time to get to know him, he has been a great friend and a solid business partner who would give me the shirt off his back if I needed it. I had to look beyond the geographical differences and view things through his perspective. Had I expected him to be like me, I never would have gotten to know him as a person, which would have been my loss. Oh, and I'm sure nothing I did offended him! Seriously, he may have had some challenges with me too, but when you focus on the other person you see things from their side of the glass.

Funny thing is I took an assessment test, which measures your aptitude and ability to market, sell and consult as an advisor. My friend took the same test at an earlier time. When the results came in, the person sharing the results had my friends test results there as well. He told me that I had one of the highest scores in the past four years and that the only one that was equal to mine was my friend.

My friend and I scored almost the same score (truth be told, his was a few points higher). Then he shared the specific categories and how we scored in each of them and we were almost exact right down the line.

CHALLENGE:

HOW OFTEN DO YOU EXPECT PEOPLE TO REACT TO A SITUATION IN THE SAME MANNER AS YOU DO? TAKE A STEP BACK AND TRY AND SEE THINGS FROM THEIR PERSPECTIVE.

We cannot really know someone unless you know what they are made of. Interesting thing here, while I thought we were so different, we weren't that far off. Brothers from a different mother? I think not. But we had a lot in common when you strip away the personalities. And had I prejudged I would have missed out.

The fact is, people are different and everyone thinks in a unique way. Our perspective is just that - OUR perspective. We see things the way we do. It is imperative to recognize that our view is only a narrow and limited perspective of the world and it's shaped by our experience in life. We cannot expect someone to see what we see because they are looking through their glasses, not ours. We must take that into account when dealing with others. Sometimes others don't understand where you are coming from. Maybe it's you that needs to change your perspective. That's opposite of what most people try to do. People look at you like you have two heads or from Mars if you don't get where they are coming from.

Once I was driving with my son along a winding, but very scenic road near my home. Around one bend there was someone riding a bike on the white line. No one else was on the road at the time, and I saw he had some room on the side so I moved over partially into the oncoming lane. I saw that he had plenty of room as I passed. But as I passed him he shouted at me and signaled that he didn't approve of my actions. Apparently he saw things from a different perspective as I did. From where I was, I gave plenty of room, but somehow he felt I was being rude. I could have stopped and made an issue with him – I lift weights every day and am experienced in martial arts. But I'll take the high road and use this story as an example of someone with a limited and self-centered view of things, plus I'm sure those funny looking shorts don't contribute to his self-esteem.

I think what makes us different is that I can project into why he feels the way he does. He is probably used to cars whizzing by and feeling as if they aren't concerned with his safety. I'll bet that he doesn't consider my perspective and probably thinks I'm just another jerk who doesn't feel the need to *"share the road man."*

If you get ten people in a room to discuss a subject, you will get no less than ten perspectives. You will agree with some of the ideas and disagree on others, but no two people will agree on everything. Some will agree more with some and less with others. That's why in our legal system we assemble juries of our peers and we give them the collective power to decide the fate of someone. I can't imagine anyone who takes the case seriously will just go along with all the opinions of another continually.

No matter what the situation is, you will be better off if you can try and appreciate where the other person is coming from and why they believe what they do. Wouldn't you want them to endeavor to see beyond their viewpoint and see your position? Of course you would. When you identify with another person's outlook, even if we don't agree, you open a more unguarded dialog and will always get further than if you refused to even consider that there was another way of looking at something.

Now your vantage point is unique and has value. You have the privilege to share it with others too. But don't think you can simply dump your opinion without hearing theirs, and I mean hearing to the end you understand it. You don't have to agree with it, but you should at least try to understand it.

When I talk to my children, they often introduce new ideas that they have learned from other centers of reference other than me. Some ideas are strange and others not as much. I try and ferret out that which is good and that which is bad according to the standards that I live by. I encourage them to listen and not judge others, but I hold the line on concepts I believe in. For example; I don't believe in discriminating against someone because they are of a different religion and encourage my children to appreciate what they feel strongly about. But when you want to take "under God" out of the pledge of allegiance, it rattles my cage. From MY perspective, this is done out of non-Christian followers or atheists pushing their idea so that they remove those "offensive" words from the pledge. Our country was founded on these principles and I believe in those words and in God. So I tell my children what I believe in and hope they comprehend my point of view. On the other hand I know that other parents feel equally as passionate about their views and will probably pass them along to their children. That is ok with me and I get where they are coming from, I just don't have to accept it as truth for me.

As long as there are other people in the world, there will be other opinions that go along with it. My point in all of this is that we don't all think alike and have a different way of looking at the issues that face us. So realize that no one is exactly like you and may have a different opinion. Imagine sitting on the other side of the table and get into what makes them think the way that they do.

Conclusion

"*It's about them*" is a theme that I personally live by and try to instill in others around me. For me its how I have been able to have tremendous success in whatever field I have been in. This philosophy has helped me differentiate myself from my competitors and allowed me to gain more insight into those around me.

I have talked to literally thousands of sales professionals across the country. There are certain traits that they have in common although they approach things with their own style. You can achieve the same level of success in any field if you model what top performers are doing. That's right, find out what they are doing and replicate it. There are things they don't do too, and I would avoid those activities as well.

Top performers also feed their mind with powerful information that arms them and sets them up to succeed in whatever they set out to do. They refuse limiting thoughts and suggestions, in fact it's repulsive to them. They have a strong belief in their ability to succeed and will expend every bit of effort in order to win. From what I have observed, they also have a knack for knowing how to connect with another individual in such a way that they want to open up to them and tell them what it is that they will buy and why.

Adoration and friendship will abound in your life when you get the focus off of yourself and get it on someone else. People will be more interested in what you have to say and will view you differently.

I'm not saying that you should never focus on yourself, because there is a time for that too. What I am saying is that when it comes to interaction with another person, it's an opportunity to understand them and glean what you can. Think of it like having blinders on in a crowded room; you can only focus on one person at a time. What would that be like?

I bumped into a vendor that my company had previously done business with and was looking for a chance to revive or salvage the relationship. Previously there was a situation where we purchased a large amount of merchandise from him and it was inferior and he didn't stand behind it. This cost us a lot of money to replace it and a lot of time too. But the thing that appealed to me was that they were closer than any other competitor and had decent product. So I liked the idea of a local vendor and was willing to give them a second chance. There was the guy I had heard about from my predecessor that had taken advantage of us. The one thing I wanted to know from him was that, if I were to give him a second chance, I needed to be sure that he would take care of us and stand behind what he sold us. Maybe he could even say something about the last transaction which I KNOW he didn't forget. I went over to his booth and introduced myself and told him that I was the one ordering now and would like to see if we could do business again, and then I waited to hear what he would say next. When he began talking it sounded like a used car salesman in a cheap suit. He didn't ask one question or try and identify with me in any way, he started rambling about their wide variety of products and great selection. It was like that screeching sound when nails go across a chalk board and it sounded like Charlie Brown's teacher – I didn't hear a word he said. He failed miserably. Needless to say he didn't address my concerns nor did he even attempt to find out how he could help me. And it was sad for him because we used to be a large customer. Instead we set up an emergency account with them and used them when it was really convenient for us, which was more like an insult than anything else.

There are so many situations where we have an opportunity to connect with someone and you never know when this will happen, so be in the habit of thinking this way. I bump into people all the time at various places and have made solid friendships at a baseball game, or football field with another parent. When you become truly interested in what makes the other person tick, you will be able to draw out a wealth of information.

Get out of your comfort zone and make it about them in your interactions with others. You can improve you communication skills by applying this principle and it will go a long way in all your relationships.

www.ingramcontent.com/pod-product-compliance
Lightning Source LLC
Chambersburg PA
CBHW022006170526
45157CB00003B/1172